Teaching Primary Children

By
FLORENCE B. LEE

Illustrated by Margaret Dugan

PHILADELPHIA
THE JUDSON PRESS

CHICAGO LOS ANGELES

TEACHING PRIMARY CHILDREN
Copyright, 1951, by The Judson Press
Eleventh Printing, April, 1960

All rights in this book are reserved. No part of the book may be reproduced in any manner without permission in writing from the publisher, except in the case of brief quotations included in a review of the book in a magazine or newspaper.

New Testament quotations are from the Revised Standard Version, copyright, 1946, by the International Council of Religious Education, and are used by permission.

This manual has been written for use by the individual teacher or superintendent. In addition, it is recommended as a textbook for a course with the same title, No. 241a: *Teaching Primary Children*, a First Series course of the Leadership Education Curriculum. Full information regarding these courses will be found in the *Leadership Education Curriculum Handbook* which may be ordered from The Judson Press.

PRINTED IN U.S.A.

CONTENTS

PAGE

FOREWORD: OBJECTIVES FOR THE RELIGIOUS
GROWTH OF PRIMARY CHILDREN 5

1. UNDERSTANDING PRIMARY CHILDREN 11
   Judy Is Six 11
   Kenneth Is Seven 12
   Marilyn and Mack Are Eight 14
   And Yet—Individual Differences 16
   The Primary Child's World 16
   Growing in Our Understanding of Children 19
   Ways of Understanding Children 20

2. MEETING THE NEEDS OF CHILDREN 25
   It Does Not Just Happen 26
   The Primary Child and God 26
   The Primary Child and Jesus 28
   The Primary Child and the Bible 29
   The Primary Child and the Church 30
   The Primary Child's Personal Christian Growth ... 31
   The Primary Child and Others 32
   A Total Task 33
   A Co-operative Task 35

3. A PLACE TO MEET 37
   The Room a Silent Teacher 38
   The Ideal Primary Room 39
   Grouping for Teaching 43
   In the Small Church 44
   Arranging the Room 46
   Let Us Begin Right Now 48
   Primary Children May Help Too 50

4. USING LESSON MATERIALS 51
   What Are Primary Graded Courses? 51
   The Bible 51

PAGE

    The Teacher's Book 53
    Pupils' Books 53
    Activity Materials 54
    Story Papers 54
    Selecting and Using Other Materials 54
    Messages to Parents 55
    Pictures 55
    Music and Songs 57
    Stories 59
    Poems 59
    Audio-Visual Materials 60
    Getting Ready to Teach 62

5. WAYS OF TEACHING 66
    Fellowship 69
    Worship 71
    Memorizing Bible Passages 74
    Litanies 75
    Choral Speaking 75

6. WAYS OF TEACHING (Continued) 77
    The Story and the Primary Child 77
    Telling the Story 77
    Primary Children May Tell Stories 78
    Dramatization 79
    Conversation 80
    Creative Activities 81
    Friendship Enterprises 83
    Trips 84
    Other Ways of Teaching 85
    Workers Needed with Primary Children 86
    The Superintendent 86
    The Pianist 87
    The Secretary 87
    The Parents 88
    The Teacher 88

HELPFUL BOOKS AND PAMPHLETS 92

FOREWORD

Objectives for the Religious Growth of Primary Children

The Child and God

A child's religious growth is conditioned primarily by his concept of God and his relationship to God. Before a child is of school age, foundations should have been laid that help him to know that God is good, that he cares for his children, and that he expects goodness of them. He will have learned that God is the Creator of this interesting and beautiful, but often puzzling, physical world.

During the primary years these concepts should expand and become more specific. The child will come to understand better how God is still at work in his world, and how we may help in this continuing creative process. His introduction to some of God's physical laws will help him to think of God as dependable as well as powerful and loving. There will be emphasis upon the fact that God is also actively at work in the world through people, and when we live according to his way of love, he can work through us to make a better and happier world for all.

Primary children should be helped to grow in their understanding of the fact that God has a wonderful plan for the life of each one of us. This plan includes life's beginning, growth and development, and the continuance of life after death. God cares for us in other ways as well, by providing good gifts that contribute to our well-being and happiness, by planning for homes and families, through people who help us and enrich our lives, and by giving us minds and wills of our own so that we can develop self-reliance and responsibility.

During their primary years the children should grow in their understanding that God's love is not for us alone, but is in equal measure for all people everywhere. He expects us to love and help one another and to help others to know of his love.

The children should be helped to know that God is a righteous God, and sin and wrongdoing are out of harmony with his will for us. They can realize that there are certain standards of right conduct which those who love God must try to meet, and they should grow in their ability to make right choices and to turn to God for help. They may begin to realize that when we fail to do this we bring unhappiness and harm to ourselves and others. They should increasingly realize that when we do wrong God is grieved, but when we ask sincerely he will forgive us and help us to do better.

There should be a growing sense of joy and satisfaction in companionship with God as the children come to appreciate his interest in all that concerns them. They should feel that God is not far away, but near by always; that he desires our love and fellowship with him through worship, and we may talk to him any time and anywhere.

The Child and Jesus

As we consider the primary child's relationship to Jesus, we appreciate the fact that the child's interest in Jesus is still largely in the facts of his matchless life on earth. His coming as a little baby, what we know of his boyhood in Nazareth, and the stories of the way in which he went about doing good continue to have great appeal. In addition to this interest in the things Jesus did, primary children should make steady growth in their ability to follow Jesus' example and teachings in their own daily living. There should be a beginning of the feeling of responsibility for sharing the story of Jesus with others.

These literal-minded children are not yet ready for mature theological interpretations, and we shall try to avoid confusing God the Father and Jesus in their minds. We will explain that Jesus, God's Son, came to show us what God is like and to help us to love God and one another. We will include some teaching of Jesus' death and resurrection, but since there is much in this experience for which primary children are not yet ready, the emphasis will be on the fact that the Bible tells us that Jesus still lives and is our Friend and Helper today. The children should realize increasingly that the work Jesus came to do is not finished, and he expects our help in carrying it forward.

In all of this teaching and learning we shall seek to build up a deep interest in and sincere love for Jesus, which we believe is the beginning of an evangelism that will bear fruit, as the child grows older, in the acceptance of Jesus Christ as personal Lord and Savior.

The Child and the Bible

Even before the children reach the Primary Department we hope they will have developed an appreciation of the Bible, and will recognize it as the special book through which God speaks to us. They should know that it tells about God and Jesus, that it is the source of well-loved stories and verses, and that its teachings help us to know how to live.

During the primary years this knowledge and understanding will increase. The children will learn more of Bible truth and Bible content, they will begin to understand something of Bible life and times, and by the time they reach the third grade they should have a beginning appreciation that the Bible tells of God's plan for the world and of the successes and failures of people in relation to it. Although the Bible is primarily an adult book, it contains much that is helpful to children, and we will choose and make thorough use during these years of those passages and verses that help them better to understand God and his purposes for them. The children should grow in their ability to use Bible truths as standards for their own conduct.

All of this enlarging knowledge and appreciation should be permeated by a spirit of enjoyment of the Bible. As the child nears junior age he should begin to know a few facts about the Bible as a book, and should have a first introduction to ways in which he himself may use it. As the Bible becomes increasingly important to the child he should begin to be aware of the importance of sharing it and its message with others.

The Child and the Church

In the preschool departments the children should have been helped to build many happy associations with the church. They will have learned something about the church building, and about many friends who work and worship together there, and they will think of the church as a special place where we learn about God and Jesus.

All of these good beginnings will be carried further in the Primary Department. The primary child should begin to think of the church not merely as a building, but as a group of adults and children who learn, work, and worship together in a happy family fellowship in which he has a part. He should become better acquainted with more church friends, both individual and groups, and he should learn more about what others do to help carry on the work of the church. He should begin to think of the church as a fellowship of those who love Jesus and seek to carry on his work, and to realize that this task is shared by churches around the world. Those parts of the church program that he can understand, both in its local and its outreach aspects, should be interpreted to him, and he should increasingly be able to participate in its life and worship. He should find ways to help, through giving, through other forms of service, and by bringing friends to share the experiences that he is enjoying.

In their last year in the Primary Department particularly, the children should begin to feel a sense of fellowship with boys and girls and men and women around the world who have similar experiences in other Christian churches.

Through such vital, satisfying, and happy experiences the primary child should begin to anticipate the time when he will be old enough to assume with understanding the full obligations of church membership.

The Child's Personal Christian Growth

Because even a child is known by what he does, we are deeply concerned that children shall grow day by day in their ability to live in more Christian ways and thus to develop strong Christian character. In the nursery and kindergarten groups opportunity for such growth will have been provided.

Primary children should make steady progress in their ability to share with others work, play, possessions, and attentions; to be obedient where obedience is necessary; to be honest and fair in all their dealings, and to be helpful and courteous and willing to work with others.

While it is important that these children begin to respect the rights, contributions, and opinions of others, it is also a part of Christian growth during these years to develop a wholesome self-respect that will lead them to be interested in discovering and making use of their own abilities, to assume some responsibility for their own well-being, and to develop more self-control and self-direction in making right choices. There should be growth in the ability to do right even when it is difficult—when it involves giving up one's own way, facing disappointments or admitting wrongdoing. The children should realize that God expects their best and will help them to achieve it. A further indication of wholesome Christian growth in primary children is the ability to recognize failures, to try again, and to look to God for help in improving.

In brief, primary children should increasingly be able to solve their problems of daily living according to the example and teachings of Jesus.

The Child and Others

The world of primary children is rapidly widening, through both personal and vicarious experiences. School with its many new contacts, experiences with neighborhood workers, exposure to visual and audio materials that bring the world to our doors, and the ease and speed of travel, have enlarged the children's knowledge of people in their own neighborhood and around the world.

As their knowledge grows the children should be helped to recognize all people, regardless of social, racial, or national differences, as brothers and sisters, and they should grow in their readiness to treat others with the respect that this ideal implies. They should develop a deeper appreciation for the contributions of other individuals and groups, and should begin to realize that though others may differ in appearance and manner from themselves, these differences serve to add richness to life, and the likenesses are after all much more important.

As the children come to realize that God's plan for his children includes the well-being and happiness of everyone, they should be helped to see that they can work with God by appreciating the viewpoints and contributions of others, and by living together in the spirit of peace and Christian fellowship.

During their years in the Primary Department the children should begin to make the acquaintance of specific areas of their church's missionary program, and should find ways of having a part in this work. This will include opportunity to share with others their knowledge of Jesus, insofar as it is possible for them to do so, for this is the heart of the Christian message.

CHAPTER 1

Understanding Primary Children

Judy Is Six

"Hello! My name is Judy. I am six years old. I am in the Primary Department now. Miss Miller is my teacher. I like my class. I like to do things, especially when I can be first. Sometimes I get tired before we are through. It's fun to be with the other boys and girls. When my teacher lets us choose, I have a hard time deciding what to do. I don't like to sit still very long. There are so many things to do and find out."

Yes, this is six-year-old Judy. She is growing more slowly now, with a lengthening of her body. She weighs approximately a pound for each inch of height. The larger muscles of her body are still much better developed than the smaller and finer muscles. Her motor control is unpredictable and erratic. Activities that require the use of the smaller muscles are difficult for her and many times she fails at them because of this physical limitation. Her heart is growing more rapidly at this period. She fatigues easily and yet she is constantly active.

Judy is alert and curious about many things, but her span of attention is not long, and she is easily diverted by the slightest provocation. One morning during the story in her Sunday school class, Judy called out, "Look! There's a bug walking upside down on the window."

Judy's vocabulary is limited. It is, however, greater than that of some six-year-old children, for Judy comes from a home in which there are many opportunities for the development of her vocabulary through reading, conversation, trips, and interesting visitors. Judy understands concrete words, but not those of abstract or symbolic meaning. She is always interested in recognizing and finding familiar words in her church school reading book. She likes to try new words, but does not always use them correctly. She talks and chatters easily, but finds it difficult to put her feelings into words. When told that her favorite uncle was coming to visit, Judy placed her hand on her chest and said, "It makes me feel all wiggly in here."

Judy dawdles and vacillates about making decisions. She hesitates for a long time over the choice of a red or blue crayon, and when she finally chooses the red one, she does not easily cancel out the other alternative. When choosing between right and wrong, she passes from one to the other in quick succession and then may not be able to decide at all, and asks someone to decide for her.

Dramatic play is very real to Judy. Through it she projects her likes and dislikes, works out her emotional tensions and moods, exposes the working of her thoughts and feelings, and even solves problems in relationships.

Judy likes active play and games. She is not much interested in competitive games or team sports. She likes running, jumping rope, playing on the gymnasium bars. She wants to be first or to win in whatever she does. She is self-assertive and aggressive.

Judy's world expanded when she started to public school. New experiences, new friends, a teacher who had authority over her actions, confinement to required schedule and tasks, are all a part of her world now. Before this, her social contacts had been limited largely to home, a few friends in the neighborhood, and perhaps the kindergarten and the church school. Now she is a member of a larger group of children with whom she must learn to live, respecting their rights and interests and property.

Kenneth Is Seven

"Miss Brown, let me unlock that cupboard door for you. Is the key stuck? I am sure that I can do it. My daddy showed me how to work the key when it gets stuck in our door at home. I can open most any door. When we get this open, will you read that story from my book again? I want to be sure I can read it when I take it home. Can we sing those two songs we sang last Sunday? I tried to find the answer to those two riddles in church school and then, you know, I got to thinking about something else and forgot all about them. There, the door is open. I knew I could do it."

This is Kenneth, who is seven years old. He likes to be near his church school teacher. He talks to impress her and to establish a personal relationship with her. While he is talking, he is setting in motion his abilities about which he likes to talk. He often boasts and exaggerates. He enjoys singing; he likes to be read to and often asks for the same story again. He is impatient with interruptions or intrusions when he is intent upon his interest and way.

Sometimes Kenneth withdraws into a world of complete self-absorption. He does not hear or respond when spoken to. These times can be very important. They help him to formulate ideas and attitudes which will lead to outward conduct.

Kenneth, at seven, is growing more slowly and steadily than he did at six. He is losing his teeth, which often causes him embarrassment. He is attaining better use of the smaller muscles of the body. He is full of energy, but still tires easily. He is often fidgety and restless.

After a year's experience in school and the first year of the Primary Department in church school, the newness of the experience has changed to one of familiarity for Kenneth. He explores to find how far the authority of the teacher reaches. The paper wad he flipped across the table at John was not only to attract attention, but to discover what Miss Brown could or would do about it. Sometimes he rebels noisily, calling names, muttering to himself, and sulking, but he does not often resort to real fighting. If this rebellion is not carried to extremes, it is not a threat to the development of Christian character, but is all a part of being seven years old.

Kenneth does not think in or understand abstract terms. He learns best in concrete situations and experiences in which he is active while he is learning. He needs adventure and opportunities through which he can achieve and do things; otherwise he will find a synthetic world of adventure in movies, the radio, comic books, and other books of questionable value.

Kenneth likes to play with other children. He demands realism in his play with less of the make-believe or pretend than before. His actions show that he reasons things out. He is learning how to live according to laws of group living. He is not quite so intent on winning as he was at six. There is still little interest in competitive, organized games. He has a growing concern about right and wrong and will assume some responsibility.

Marilyn and Mack Are Eight

"I am Marilyn, and this is my brother, Maclynn. We are both eight years old because we are twins. We like to read and go on trips. Miss Walker, our Sunday school teacher, took us to visit a missionary who had a whole collection of dolls from other lands. We sure did like them. We girls formed a doll club in our class. The boys wouldn't join. I have a collection of paper dolls. I went home when I was almost at school yesterday because I had left my paper dolls scattered all over my room and Mother had said that she would burn them up if she found them scattered around again. I had to hurry, but I made it all right."

"Marilyn is always telling people that my name is Maclynn. Well, it is, but I like Mack. I liked the trip to the missionary's house, but she had some knives, books, and pictures that were a lot more interesting than those old dolls. You should see my bottle tops and marbles. The gang in our room at school has a Toles Club. You see that is the first two letters of tops and the last two except "s" of marbles, and "s" is on both words. It is a sort of a secret name. We have fun trading with each other. Only members can come to our meetings, but we can trade with anyone. We don't allow girls in the Toles Club. They are always fussing and want to dress up. If they get hurt, they cry."

Yes, Marilyn and Mack are eight years old. Their physical growth is still steady and slow. Their hands are growing larger. Their arms are lengthening. The large muscles of the body are developing, and there is more rapid and consistent development of the smaller muscles also. They have better eye and hand co-ordination. Permanent teeth fill in the gaps which the lost baby teeth had left. The eight-year-old looks more mature and does not tire as easily as the six- and seven-year-old children.

Marilyn and Mack have grown more mature mentally, also. They can read well, and do read many books, newspapers, comics, and magazines spontaneously and for pleasure. Books of adventure and travel, and books about other lands and peoples, interest them. They are learning to write script instead of the manuscript writing used before, but they still revert to printing when tired or in a hurry. They will write letters and like especially to receive them. Their vocabularies have grown so that they understand and use words correctly.

The twins have become time-conscious. They can tell time quite accurately when it is related to something they want to see, hear, or do. At other times they need to be reminded of time. Even though they are interested in ancient times and in things that happened in times far past, their sense of chronology is undeveloped. For instance, they often confuse characters and events of the Old and New Testaments.

Their play and their explorations in their neighborhood now cover a much greater distance. They may come to Sunday school alone. They sometimes make trips to the store alone to take care of errands for Mother or to make purchases of some desired possessions.

The twins' social development has taken new turns. They are friendly and interested in people, but are careless, argumentative, and impatient with those of the same age but opposite sex. Clubs, secret groups, and gangs become the pattern of group living. These groups usually are not well organized and do not last long. Boys and girls have "best friends," usually of the same sex, and they are intolerant toward another child of the same or opposite sex who intrudes in this friendship. They like to play team games, and are boisterous, rough, and often daring in their play. They respond to adult supervision of group activities.

Marilyn and Mack are interested in money and what it will buy. They may spend all their money on some desired object. Often they are very generous in treating their "best friends." They are developing a property sense, but need help in attaining an understanding of values. They need guidance in the care and use of their possessions. Training in stewardship is important at this age.

The twins are more capable of self-evaluation and of thinking things through than they were at seven. They make a decision more easily concerning something of importance to them. They have a growing responsibility for their choices and acceptance of the consequences of those choices. However, they are quick to place the blame on someone else for starting trouble or wrong action. They are prone to make excuses and offer alibis. One has the feeling that they are conscious that they are making excuses, and will be self-critical and honest under careful guidance.

And Yet—Individual Differences

Judy, Kenneth, Marilyn, and Mack—these are primary children. They have many traits and characteristics common to their particular age, yet we must remember that no two children are exactly alike. No two children will see and respond to a situation in exactly the same way. Each child is a person with individual capacities and limitations. His family and other home influences, his neighborhood, his past experiences, his school, the culture into which he was born and lives, and many other factors have made him what he is. These factors are not identical for any two children, even twins. Their inheritance, environment, and experiences determine their response to a situation. It is important that teachers recognize individual differences, respecting each child as a person, helping each to develop at his own rate and according to his capacities for growth.

The Primary Child's World

The primary child's world is an expanding one. Each day, week, and month brings new persons, objects, and experiences into his environment. He wants to explore these and experiment with them.

The primary child's world is an active one. One teacher described her primary children as perpetual motion machines. They are not satisfied to sit, think, and listen for long periods of time. They want to do things. They do not want to talk about the lesson; they want to act it out or experiment in living situations with the truths it teaches. A class of primary children was planning a project. "If we are going to do this in the very best way, we will need to co-operate," said the teacher. It suddenly occurred to her that the children might not know the meaning of the word "co-operate." She asked, "What does the word 'co-operate' mean?"

"It means to work together," Richard answered.

"That is right. Now let us talk about ways in which we should co-operate in our project," continued the teacher.

"Aw, what's the use of talking about it? Why don't we just do it?" came the impatient response from Frank.

The primary child's world is one of imitation. Reasoning has not fully flowered. Much is learned by trial and error, but the child often does what is suggested by the actions of some other person, either child or adult. When he sees a plan of action, he follows it. He reflects many adult actions, attitudes, and words, and these help to mold his conduct and personality. It has been said that character is more contagious at this age than at any other time.

The primary child's world contains tasks and work that are within his capacities and that he can complete with a sense of satisfaction and achievement. These provide a growing edge for his increasing independence. Respect for the rights and property of others, an understanding of the need for rules for the good of all, and respect for the right kind of authority must be a part of his training; otherwise this independence will develop into an undesirable individualism.

The primary child's world is a social world. These children want to play and work with other children. They want to be accepted by the group; their security and happiness are dependent upon this acceptance. Group standards and codes of conduct are sometimes stronger influences than the training and pressure of adults. A second-grade class met in a small room equipped only with folding chairs. The chairs were unstable and too small for the children. Under the movements of restless, active seven-year-olds, the chairs sometimes "scooted" out from under them. The teacher realized the reason for this, but she also knew that she must help the children to be more careful for the greater good of the group. She talked with the children, and they decided that if a boy or girl could not be careful and sit on the chair, he could just sit on the floor when the chair "scooted" out, and he went down. All went well for the remainder of that class period. The next Sunday, during the story, "bang" went a chair, and Glenn found himself sitting on the floor. The teacher paused, but said not a word. Glenn looked from child to child, all the way around the circle. Not a word was spoken. Glenn remained on the floor until the close of the class period. Seldom was there an interruption from a "scooting" chair after that, and the matter never required further conversation. The children had made the decision and each child strove to stay in the good graces of the group by abiding by the group decision.

The primary child's world is a world of play. Free and spontaneous, individually and in small groups, in larger groups, loud and boisterous, quiet and then rough-and-tumble, imitative and then creative—these are some of the play patterns of primary children. Dramatic play is extremely important during these years, for through dramatic play the children work out their problems, clarify their understanding of their experiences, experiment with ways of living, and find release for emotional tensions and pressures.

Katherine (six years old) and Joan (eight) had been disappointed in a trip to the zoo because an unexpected household task had kept their mother from taking them. Katherine, crying, and Joan, talking in undertones, resentfully slammed the door as they went out to the yard to play. Housekeeping with dolls was the chosen activity. Katherine's doll was soon sick unto death, with a repentant mother sorrowing because she had not taken her child to the zoo before the child died. Joan's doll ran away to make her mother sorry for being so mean to her. Soon all the resentment was gone, and the emotions had been worked off or released through dramatic play. Two happy children ran into the house calling, "Mother, if we help you this afternoon, would you take us to the zoo this evening, maybe?"

The primary child's world is a literal, concrete world. Their vocabularies are growing during these years, but are still limited. Their reasoning power is developing, but is still immature. The world becomes confusing to them if words and ideas which they cannot understand are used with them. An inexperienced teacher loved the hymn, "Lead On, O King Eternal," and thought that it would be excellent to use with her primary children. To her amazement she discovered that some of the children were singing, "Lead on, O King eat turtles." They did not know what the word "eternal" meant. It was an abstract word and they were literal-minded. So they sang words which had concrete meaning and which sounded like "eternal." While their ability to reason is developing, they still think and express themselves concretely. Often they find it difficult to express their thoughts and feelings because they cannot find the right words. They do not understand symbols or words of symbolic meaning, or abstract ideas. Object lessons or other similar methods of teaching are usually ineffective, because the child's interest is centered on the object or on how the thing works and he does not grasp the symbolic teaching.

The primary child's world is one in which vivid imagination plays a large part. Pretense and make-believe hold sway. As he grows toward eight years old, he begins to sort out the difference between fact and fancy, to distinguish between truth and imagination. We do not want to repress his imagination, but to direct it into creative, constructive channels. Creative imagination is the beginning of the genius of the poet, the artist, the inventor, the scientist, the builder, and the composer.

Primary children are curious about the world in which they live. Their senses are alert. They investigate, examine, explore, and question. The "where" and "when" questions of the younger child become the "why" and "how" questions of the primary child. When a bus pulled off the road and stopped, the four-year-old child asked, "Where are we?" The seven-year-old asked, "Why did we stop?" Questions should be answered patiently, honestly, and frankly. If the teacher does not know the answer, an honest "I don't know, but let us see if we can find the answer" will satisfy the child. When the child's questions cannot be answered because he cannot understand or because we ourselves do not fully understand, our reply may need to be: "I don't understand all about it. There are many things which we don't understand. Perhaps sometime someone will find the answer to that question. Or perhaps, as we learn more, we may discover the answer."

Growing in Our Understanding of Children

A teacher who is growing in her understanding of children will recognize each child as an individual. Her plans for teaching will be made with each child in mind, taking into consideration his unique characteristics as well as the traits common to children of his age. Janice is a natural leader; she will need help in developing her powers of leadership for the greatest good of all. Dan is shy and a dreamer; it will take skill and patience to lead him into active participation in group activities. Dorothy is always on the fringe of things, never wholly accepted by the other children yet always striving to be one of the group; she needs guidance in finding her place happily.

An understanding teacher accepts each child without prejudice. She sees and feels the potential in each one. Her love and concern includes all, regardless of economic status, race, religious background, physical or mental limitations. Every child is loved by God, and needs to be led into closer relationship with him.

An understanding teacher keeps an inquiring, open mind and heart. She will be eager to learn new things about the children and from them. When her heart and mind are open to the children, they will reveal many anxieties, hopes, problems, joys, and desires. They will help her to see a confusing world through their eyes. When she sees, feels, and thinks as a child does, there will be no condemnation or hasty judgment, but only loving sympathy and help.

An understanding teacher's mind and heart will be open to new concepts of eternal truths; she will have a maturing relationship to God through Jesus Christ, and will discover ways through which she can reveal eternal truths and the Christlike way of life to the child. At the center of all her plans and prayers will be a deep concern for each child and his spiritual growth. She will have a sense of being a "fellow workman for God" as she reveals his purpose and plan to her primary children.

Ways of Understanding Children

We know that none of us has a perfect understanding of our children. We want to continue to grow in understanding. How may we do this?

1. *Reading.* We may learn to understand primary children by reading about them. Many excellent books and magazine articles on child psychology are available in church and public libraries.

Books *for* children, written by those who know and love children, will give insight into child life. Books and stories of fiction *about* children will provide pleasant reading, and likewise will give insight into child life, if written by those who know children and their ways.

2. *Study Courses.* Attendance and participation in study classes, conferences, institutes, and workshops will help the teacher to understand the children she teaches. Study courses, including the home study plan, are of special value and are offered by most denominations.

The Fellowship of Children's Workers, or some similar service of the Department of Children's Work in your denomination, offers another means of help and guidance for your growth as a teacher.

You may secure information concerning these plans by writing to the Leadership Education Division at your denominational headquarters.

3. *Being with Children.* Really to understand children, one must be with them. A teacher needs to go to a child with an inquiring mind and learn from him. It is illuminating to watch children at play, but it is more enlightening to be accepted as one of them and play with them. A play period with your primary children will reveal interests, needs, and behavior that must be guided into better ways. Wilma, who was six, had talked glibly in class about sharing and taking turns, but at a party in her home to which her Sunday school teacher had been invited, her actions showed she did not know the first principles of sharing and taking turns.

As we look at pictures and read books with children, we catch their freshness of vision, lack of prejudice, sense of humor, and spirit of joy and hope. A teacher noted that Tommy, who had just reached the age of six, went again and again to look at a picture which had been placed on a low table. The picture showed the boy Jesus standing on the hilltop at Nazareth. Curious as to what Tommy was thinking and feeling, the teacher paused by him the next time he went to the picture. Tommy looked up at her and said: "I sure feel sorry for Jesus. He must have gotten lots of stickers in his feet." The teacher knew that to Tommy, Jesus was a real boy who had had experiences, joys, and difficulties, even as he did.

Taking a walk or going on a trip with a child is a rewarding experience when it is an adventure together. On such an adventure an alert teacher will discover wonderings, inaccurate knowledge or concepts, expanding interests. There will be moments of awe and wonder which may lead to informal worship. A group of primary children paused before a flower garden that was a riot of color and variety. After a pause filled with awe and wonder, Dick said, "No one could do that but God, could he?" Before the teacher could reply, Evelyn said, "I think we ought to say thank you to God right now." Heads were bowed and the "thank you" was voiced.

Observe children as they play, work, and worship in the church school classes and department. Dale's actions and attitudes puzzled Mr. Kent. The boy would work and co-operate in the activities wholeheartedly for a number of Sundays. Then he would seem to go off on a tangent. He would be unruly or passively nonco-operative for a Sunday or two. Because Mr. Kent wanted to find the cause, he visited Dale's home, his public school, and even made little excursions with Dale. He watched Dale with the other children. He learned that the boy's best friend was Roger. Mr. Kent thought that he had the answer to his concern when he went over the attendance records of the two boys for the past year. However, he wanted to be sure, so he continued his observation for six months more. Dale was regular in attendance; Roger was irregular. Dale's bad days were the ones when Roger was absent. He was insecure in his relations with other children and dependent upon Roger. When Roger was absent, Dale sought the approval and attention of the others by unworthy conduct. Mr. Kent was ready now to help Dale find security in better ways, for he had discovered the cause of his conduct through observation and study, and by visiting in the home and with Dale.

4. *Visiting in the Home.* Calling in the home is essential for understanding the child's personality and development. A call in the home should bring rich rewards for the child, the teacher, and the parents. The Christian training of primary children must be a joint responsibility of home and church. This responsibility calls for knowledge of the child and his needs and of the goals for his Christian training.

We are interested in the child. We will learn about him from his parents. We will discover their aspirations and hopes for him. We will be sensitive to their pride in his abilities and achievements, and sympathetic with their disappointment in his limitations or failures. We will listen as well as talk. We will recount growth and achievements which we have noted in his church school work.

Some of our calls will be made when the child is at home. He likes to have his teacher come to his home. It gives him status in the family. If there have been problems at church school, however, the call may mean anxiety and tension for fear that teacher may tell. Plan with the child for the call, include him in the conversation when you go, and approve that which you can approve. No matter what a child has said or done, an understanding teacher can find a good attitude, the lovely expression of a thought, or some fine act to approve. When making the first call it often helps a less-experienced teacher to take with her a copy of the parents' material which most denominations publish with their primary courses.

Explanations of work and sharing of experiences will help the parents to discover ways in which they can supplement the work of the church school. The teacher will discover ways in which she can aid and work with the parents. Together they will think of their common objectives in the Christian training of the child and will plan to work together for him.

5. *Visiting the Public School.* A visit to the public school classes of your children will be well worth your time. It will not only help you to discover methods and materials of teaching, but will also help you to understand the child as he responds and reacts in the school situation. It will help you understand more fully his capacities and limitations.

For Further Study

1. Suppose a mother brought two children, one six and the other eight years of age, to your Primary Department and requested that they be placed in the same class. How would you explain your reasons for insisting on placing the younger one in the first-year class and the older one in the third-year class?

2. Choose one of the children in your class and write your findings concerning him. Make separate sections for his abilities, limitations, interests, and needs. In each case note what you have found out by reading, by being with him, and by calling in the home.

Perhaps you will want to make such a chart for each child in your class and keep it over the period of time that he is a member of your group. If so, you will wish to add notes about his achievements or failures, giving the date for each, describing it, and noting what you think is the cause. Be sure to include a record of your plans for helping him, and evidences of spiritual growth that you observe.

3. Having discovered some of the needs and characteristics of primary children, evaluate the ways in which your church is meeting these. What changes will you make?

4. List as many reasons as possible for the differences in children. What are some of the implications of this list for your work as a teacher?

CHAPTER 2

Meeting the Needs of Children

MRS. PORTER had been reading *Alice in Wonderland* to Jane, who was seven years old. After Jane was in bed, Mrs. Porter sat down at her desk to work on the lesson and plans for her primary class. For some reason the plans wouldn't work out right. Some sentences she had just read came back to her mind.

When Alice in Wonderland met the Cheshire cat, she asked, "Would you tell me, please, which way I ought to walk from here?"

"That depends a good deal on where you want to get to," said the cat.

"I don't care much where," said Alice.

"Then it doesn't matter which way you walk," said the cat.

Suddenly Mrs. Porter realized that she was not clear in her thinking as to "where she wanted to get to" in her work with the children. Her plans seemed aimless and without direction. She began to define her objectives: "I want my primary children to grow in Christian character. I want them to learn some Bible verses and know some Bible stories. I want them to be Christian and have the abundant life which Jesus came to give." Thinking that at last she knew "where she wanted to get to," Mrs. Porter turned to her work. As she tried to bring together her plans and objectives, she discovered that her objectives were too general to be of much value for the specific plans which she must make for next Sunday. They seemed far removed from the things she wanted to do in the weeks immediately ahead.

"I don't care much where." "Then it doesn't matter which way you walk." Again the conversation between Alice and the cat came to mind. The faces of some of her children flashed into Mrs. Porter's thoughts. Could it be possible that many of their class enterprises had had little value for the children because their teacher had not had a clear sense of direction? With this thought came the realization that she had been mistaking means for ends. Methods and materials were not the ends, but only the means of reaching the ends. Mrs. Porter's greatest need was an understanding of what her objectives should be and their relationship to what she did in each session with the children.

Mrs. Porter recalled that several weeks ago at a children's workers institute she had received a pamphlet on *Objectives for the Christian Education of Children.* After a search through several desk drawers, she found it, and set to work to study it. She would know "where she wanted to go," and then it "would matter which way she walked."

It Does Not Just Happen

The most wholesome and most rewarding Christian growth does not "just happen." It is carefully planned for and attained through understanding and working toward objectives that have been chosen to meet the spiritual needs of persons. A growing Christian experience will not "just happen" for primary children. Because they have listened quietly to a story, made a diorama of Nazareth, or can repeat Psalm 100 does not necessarily mean that the children's spiritual needs have been met or that they have grown in ability to live in Christian ways. Objectives must be stated and interpreted in specific terms for each age group. Objectives that are suitable for adults are not suitable for primary children, unless the adults have not advanced beyond the primary level in their Christian growth! However, objectives for the guidance of primary children are basic steps toward a maturing adult Christian life.

It is essential that each teacher of primary children study and understand the six objectives of Christian education, for these are the ways in which a child of six, seven, or eight years should develop in his relationships with God, Jesus, the Bible, the church, himself, and other people. Much of the success or failure of the teacher's work will be determined by her understanding of these objectives and how closely she relates all materials and methods which she may use to them.

The Primary Child and God

Basic concepts and foundations of the primary child's relationship with God have been laid in the home, the Nursery and Kindergarten Departments of the church school and in other situations before he enters the Primary Department. Unless he is one of the many children who have had no guidance at all, he should know that God is good and feel that he cares for his children. The child should realize that God expects goodness of him. He will have learned that God has created the world and given it to us to enjoy.

During the three years that he is in the Primary Department these concepts should take on more specific meaning. There should be a growing appreciation of the fact that God is the Creator of all and that he works through established laws and is still at work in his world. The child will discover ways in which he can work for God in this continuing creative process. Bible verses and stories will be used to help the child learn this, but his deepening appreciation of God, the Creator, will develop best through real experiences with nature under the guidance of a wise, sympathetic teacher.

The primary child should learn that God is powerful, loving, and dependable. He should learn that God is actively at work through those people who live according to his purpose and plan for them, as well as through the laws of nature. Primary children should be helped to know that God's way is the way of love, and that God has a purpose and plan for each person, which includes his growth and development and a continuing life after death. They will discover that homes, families, and other helpers who contribute to their happiness are a part of God's plan for them. They will recognize that their bodies, minds, and wills are God's gifts, and that God expects each one to care for and use these gifts wisely in making right choices and developing responsibility.

During the primary years the child will be helped to feel that God is a righteous God. He will learn that God loves him at all times and that he should grow in his desire to do right and fulfill God's purpose for his life. His knowledge and understanding of right and wrong should expand, and his ability to make right choices should be strengthened. When the child has done wrong, he will recognize that his choice was not in accord with God's plan for him, that wrong choices and acts grieve God, and bring unhappiness to himself and others. The child will come to realize that God forgives when we are truly sorry and turn to him for help. The child should feel a renewal of fellowship with God as he tries to do better.

The primary child should increasingly feel the nearness of God and God's desire for his constant love and fellowship with him through worship. The child will grow in his understanding that he may talk to God any time and anywhere. Perhaps in no other relationship with God is the spirit and example of the teacher more potent. At the close of a prayer time, a six-year-old child said to his teacher: "How can you say such nice things when you pray? I thought I could touch God."

The child's experience in the church school should help him to know that God cares for and loves all people everywhere, and that through people who love and understand one another God works to help people everywhere to know him and live as his children.

The Primary Child and Jesus

In the preschool years the child has been interested in stories of the birth and boyhood of Jesus, and stories of the helpful, kind things which Jesus did for others. The child has grown in his understanding and appreciation of Jesus as Friend of all, and one who helps people to know what God is like.

The primary child's interest is still largely in facts about Jesus and his life on earth, but primary children must go beyond this. The primary child should learn that Jesus is God's Son. He will accept this without deep theological interpretations or explanations which only confuse him because of his immaturity in reasoning and understanding. Primary teachers will help the children to know that Jesus came to teach and show what God is like. The children should grow in their attitudes of love and appreciation for Jesus as one who reveals God's will and purpose to them. They will grow in their understanding that Jesus was an expression of God's love and came to help us love God and one another.

Primary children will grow in their realization that as "Jesus of Nazareth . . . went about doing good" (Acts 10:38), so he expects them to be his helpers and have a part in carrying on his work of kindness, helpfulness, and love in the world. They will come to know that service to Jesus means service to others.

Some teachings of Jesus' death and resurrection will be given, but since most primary children have very limited ideas and experiences with death, teachers must deal with these questions as they arise. Emphasis should be on the fact that Jesus still lives as their Friend and Helper.

Primary children are not ready, except in a few cases, to make a decision to accept Jesus as their Savior and Lord, but we, as teachers, will keep constantly in our minds, hearts, and prayers, the knowledge that all that we do and say as we guide these children in their growing relationship to Jesus is preparation for that time of supreme decision.

The Primary Child and the Bible

Before the child enters the Primary Department, he should know that the Bible is a special book through which God speaks to us. He should know that it teaches about God and Jesus and helps children know how to live. The child will have learned a few simple Bible verses and stories which will have been used over and over again.

During the primary years the number of Bible verses and stories which the child hears and knows will be increased. He will enjoy learning and using in the department worship carefully chosen Bible verses and longer passages, such as Psalm 100 and Luke 2:8-14. During the third year of the Primary Department the child may begin to read some of these familiar verses and passages for himself. He will enjoy telling and retelling these Bible stories and will learn through the experience of dramatizing them.

Bible backgrounds, customs, and peoples are of interest to primary children, particularly to the older ones. So Bible truths, verses, and stories take on new meaning. As seven-year-old Harold placed on a table the model which he had made of a Nazareth house, he looked up at his teacher and said, "Now I know how those friends could let the man down through the roof to see Jesus and not fall off. The roof wasn't pointed at all. It was flat."

As the primary child comes to the third grade, he will learn a few facts about the Bible as a book. He will begin to use it in ways according to his ability. He should be led to feel the importance of this unique book which tells of God and Jesus and gives rules for living, and have real opportunities of sharing it and its message with others.

There should be opportunities for the primary child to use and enjoy these Bible verses and stories in other situations. The family worship or devotional period in the home will provide one of these opportunities. A letter or a visit to the home is most helpful in acquainting the parents with the Bible passages or stories which the child has memorized or can read. As the home and church co-operate in helping the child to appreciate and use the Bible, he begins to see its value as a guidebook for everyday living and not a book for Sunday use only.

The Primary Child and the Church

Out of his happy experiences in the Nursery and Kindergarten Departments in the church school the child will have learned

something of the church as a place where people worship and work together as they learn about God and Jesus.

The primary child should move on from his concept of the church as a building or place to an understanding that the church is a fellowship of loving, helpful persons who follow and serve Jesus. This idea of the church as a Christian fellowship can come only out of rich experiences in such a fellowship. Lois, aged three and a half, when passing the church building, had remarked to her mother, "There is my dear old sweet Sunday school." At seven Lois said to her mother after Sunday school one morning: "You know, Mother, I forgot that I was even in the church building this morning. There seemed to be so many happy people everywhere that it made me feel all happy too. I think everybody likes me." Happy experiences in the Primary Department with the other children and the teachers had helped Lois to have a "sense of belonging" to a worth-while fellowship. This idea should be carefully fostered and developed during the years that Lois is in the Primary Department. The church as the body of Christ is beyond her understanding at this age, but Lois can grow in her appreciation of Jesus and in the understanding that the church is made up of friends and followers of Jesus who are working together to share his message with others.

Happy times with the minister and other church workers should be a part of the child's experiences. He should learn what individual members and groups do to carry on the work of the church. Stewardship of giving takes on richer meaning during the primary years as the children learn of the needs of the church for money in its local program and missionary outreach. During a trip through the church building and a conference with the minister and church secretary, a group of primary children discovered twenty-four needs which their church had for money. In the discussion which followed, they talked of ways in which they could help, not alone by bringing their gifts of money, but by helping with their time and abilities. So they provided flowers for the chancel once each month. They planted bulbs in a bare corner of the churchyard in order that it might be attractive and beautiful in the spring. They decided to use church envelopes for their offering. These children were growing in churchmanship and were beginning to plan and look forward to the time when they would be old enough to become responsible church members.

There will be opportunities for the primary children to grow through the fellowship of worship in their classes and department. Occasionally the children will worship with the church family in the sanctuary.

The Primary Child's Personal Christian Growth

Children six, seven, and eight years old should begin to have a sense of responsibility for their own conduct. They should grow in their ability to make choices according to Christian principles and teachings, and be willing to see and accept the consequences of their choices even when this means unhappiness and disappointment.

Primary children should carry through to completion activities which they have started, providing these activities have been wisely chosen and are within their ability. This helps them to grow in dependability and find satisfaction in a task well done.

Primary children should be growing in their ability to share their work, play, and possessions with others, thinking of the happiness of others before their own selfish desires. Honesty and fairness in their dealings with others should become a part of their daily living. They should grow in their respect for the rights, opinions, and contributions of other people. They will learn to be obedient when obedience is necessary. They should increasingly show friendliness, thoughtfulness, and courtesy to others without having to be reminded to do so.

Primary children should be helped to develop a wholesome self-respect, to recognize and make good use of their abilities, and to grow in self-control as children of God. These children should learn that God's laws demand obedience and that God expects them to work with him in caring for themselves. They should know when they have failed to live at their best or have sinned. They will be guided to look to God for help, and not only will they desire to do better, but increasingly they will achieve greater self-control and the ability to do right in the light of the example and teachings of Jesus.

The teacher must realize that the most wholesome development of Christian character comes from controls and motivation within the child. It takes less time and is comparatively easy to make a child do the thing which we wish. It takes a long time and is a more difficult process to help the child develop those inner controls that result in personal Christian growth.

The Primary Child and Others

In a study group a primary teacher asked: "How do children learn to appreciate and understand other persons? My boys and girls are always kind and share with Juna, but they have not accepted him. There is a bit of smugness and condescension in their attitudes." This teacher had recognized that helping children to grow in a right relationship to others was more than outward conformity to "expected" conduct. What the child thinks and feels about the other person is as important as what he does.

The primary child's world is an expanding one. It includes many types of persons and experiences with them. Indeed it is "one world," and even if the primary child never left his home, the magazines, radio, newspapers, visitors, and television would bring the world to his door. How do we want him to think, feel, and act toward others in his world?

The primary child should appreciate first the individual children in his church school, play, and public school groups. Then he should grow in his realization that God loves all people. He should realize that God's plan includes their welfare and happiness. He should grow in his readiness and ability to treat others with understanding and respect. He should be helped to value persons as persons, recognizing their abilities, good qualities, and contributions. There may be dislike for the wrong which a person has done, but love for the person. The primary child will discover and recognize differences in manners, appearances, customs, and beliefs of other people, but it is the likenesses that should be emphasized.

The primary child should learn about and share in the missionary enterprises of his church at home and abroad. We cannot have the true feeling of brotherhood without the deeds of brotherhood. Thinking, feeling, and acting must go hand in hand if the child is to grow in Christian relationships with others.

The teacher and parents of children cannot give a mere lip service to the great fundamentals of our faith, such as belief in God as Father, Christ as Savior, and Christian brotherhood. They must exemplify these if they are to inspire children to Christian living. If teachers and parents are friendly and generous, children will tend to be so. As teachers and parents are unprejudiced and consistently show love to others, children follow their example. Let us to the best of our ability and with God's help live together as Christians with all people at all times and in all situations.

A Total Task

Our objectives, the needs of children, and our materials and methods are all bound up together for effective teaching.

It is impossible to guide the child in only one area of Christian growth at a time.

A class of second-grade children who had attained little skill in working together had presented many problems to its teacher. The unit of lessons had as its objective to help the children grow in understanding and appreciation of God, the giver of every good and perfect gift. While this was the major objective, the teacher was aware also of the children's need to learn to co-operate and work with each other in satisfying ways. Consequently many activities were planned that would help the children learn about God and also find satisfaction in co-operative endeavors. The children decided to make a springtime book of pictures and Bible verses to share with another department. They were to choose Bible verses and draw pictures to illustrate them. Each child might have made one page for the book, but in order to provide an opportunity for growth in co-operation, the teacher guided their planning so that they would work in groups of two, one child printing the verse on a piece of colored construction paper and the other child drawing the picture on white paper which when finished would be mounted above the verse. The teacher had printed the Bible verses on slips of paper from which each group was to choose one. At the close of the session, the primary superintendent came to the teacher and said, "What do you suppose two of your boys said as they were leaving?"

"Who were the boys?" asked the teacher.

"Arthur and Billy," replied the superintendent.

"No telling what they said. They are my problem children. What was it?"

"Arthur said to me: 'You ought to see the book we are making to help the kindergarten children learn some of the things we know about God. I printed the verse and Billy drew the picture. It's a swell book. We sure do work together in Mrs. Thomas' class.'"

"I do feel encouraged," the teacher answered. "I have been trying to help my children learn to co-operate for the past six months, through every series of lessons that we have had, even when the major emphasis was on another objective."

We work toward our purposes and objectives through all that happens in the session. The worship experiences, the fellowship between teachers and children, the incidental conversation, the atmosphere and appearance of the room all make their contribution to the children's Christian development. There should be unity and purposeful planning in all that the teacher does for and with the children.

A Co-operative Task

Most parents want to do their share to carry on the things done in the church school class. They want to understand and work with the teachers of their children. But how can they help us fulfill our objectives in specific ways and at suitable times, if they do not know what those objectives are? And our one hour of teaching each week will prove ineffective if we know nothing of what is happening to the child the remainder of the week. Parents and teachers must work together for the sake of the child. Hence, the importance of viewing the work to be done as a co-operative task, and of making it such in fact as well as in theory.

Parents often do not know what is being done in the church school and the teachers do not know what goes on in the homes. A friendly visit in the home of each child by his teacher will do much to make the parents feel that the home is of first importance in this task of building Christian character in the child. The teacher should also help the parents feel that the church school wants to help them in this task.

Parents may be invited to visit the primary class or department at which time the children will share with them some of the work they have been doing. The teacher will find opportunity to help the parents understand the purposes related to the work, as well as tell them how they may strengthen these objectives through other activities in the home.

All that happens within the church fellowship has its effect upon the children of the church. Meeting the needs of children is a church task.

A harmonious fellowship among the members of the church family, kind words, thoughtful deeds, cheerful greetings, and radiant faith exemplify the way of Christ to the children and challenge them to follow his way of life. The child hears words of praise and kindness about others and he begins to look for the good rather than the evil in persons. He sees people practicing Christianity and he is challenged to live as a Christian. A child grows best in a friendly, natural atmosphere.

For Further Study

1. Evaluate the hymns used in your Primary Department. How do they interpret God to the children? Are these ideas of God the ones described in the section, "The Primary Child and God"?

2. Study three pictures from the picture sets used with the graded lessons. List ideas of Jesus which the pictures would give to children.

3. Discuss the difference between telling a Bible story and applying it to the child's experience, and using a Bible story to interpret or enrich an experience.

4. Consider your objectives for primary children. Does the church's total program help reach these objectives? How?

5. Study one of the pamphlets or books listed in the bibliography (see page 92) that you would like to take to the homes of your children. Plan how you would approach and discuss it with the parents.

6. What experiences does your church provide for primary children to relate them to the total church program?

7. Study the purposes of the next unit of study for your class. How are these purposes related to one or more of our general objectives for the Christian education of primary children?

CHAPTER 3

A Place to Meet

Two street urchins dropped into a beautiful church and one remarked, "Ain't it nice in here; it just makes you feel like you want to be good."

Upon Patricia's return from Sunday school, her mother asked, "How did you like your new Sunday school?"

"Oh, I guess it was all right, but it was kind of messy and didn't look very nice," Patricia replied in an uninterested manner.

One end of the vestibule of a one-room church had been partitioned off and the primary teacher and children had arranged the space for their class. They called it their "chapel." A simulated stained-glass rose window placed over a clear glass window, an appropriate picture, a low table on which were an open Bible and the offering plates, and a bowl of ivy formed the center of beauty or worship. Leon had brought his friend, Jack, to the church on their way home from school. As the boys stepped into the "chapel" Leon said nothing, just paused on the threshold for a few moments. Turning to Jack he said, "This is our children's chapel. Isn't it quiet and lovely?"

In another church, Jimmy, who was seven, had invited his mother to visit his department, but had qualified his invitation with the remark, "If there is too much to do when we get there, I won't have time to show you around."

When Jimmy and his mother arrived at the primary room on Sunday morning, Jimmy stepped up to the bulletin board, read the list of things to be done, and then said to his mother, "Would you please come to visit next Sunday, Mother, instead of today? We have a lot to do this morning."

"Yes, Son, I will stay next Sunday when you have more time." Jimmy's mother lingered for a moment at the door. No wonder Jimmy was always eager to come to Sunday school. The room was light and attractively arranged. She glanced at her watch. It was fifteen minutes before time to begin. Yet already the session had started, for groups of children were busily at work on various activities. The room seemed to say: "Come, get busy. There is interesting work to do here."

The Room a Silent Teacher

Have you paused to think what your primary room may be saying to your children? Stand on the threshold and look in. Imagine that you are six, seven, or eight years old. What does the room say to you? Is there a place in it that invites you to enter and in quiet reverence worship God? Does it say, "Come, this is a place for children to work together. The chairs and tables are just the right height for you. There is a place for your work materials. The pictures have been chosen with you in mind. And peek into the low shelves. There are pictures, books, crayons, Bibles, scissors, and other materials which you will need for your work. Of course you will want to keep them as orderly as they are now."

Do the orderliness, beauty, arrangement, lighting, warmth, and cleanliness of the room make you feel that this is a good place to be? The room should say: "There will be freedom for you here. You may express yourself through creative work. You will have freedom to work with and for the other boys and girls and teachers. You may try out your own ideas and experiment in ways of living."

The general appearance and care of the church building speak to the children as they approach it. A small, well-painted frame building with clean, clear-glass windows, neat lawns, clean sidewalks, flowers, and shrubbery may say more to a child than a larger brick structure with stained-glass windows broken here and there, weather-beaten doors, littered yards and walks. The former says: "I am important to the people who come here to worship God. Religion has first place in their lives. They give and work that their place of worship and fellowship may be attractive and demand the respect of all." The latter says, "The people do not think I am important enough to take care of me and make me a place of beauty and loveliness."

Primary children learn that they are regarded as an important part of the church family if adequate rooms and equipment are provided for them. In an issue of a denominational publication, C. H. Benson wrote, "Jesus put the child in the midst; most Sunday schools put him in the basement." Have suitable rooms and equipment taught your primary children that they are "in the midst" of the church fellowship? Have their needs for adequate space and equipment been taken care of?

An orderly, clean room will teach responsibility and orderliness to the children. Such a room will enlist the interest of the children in keeping it that way. It will help the children feel that their Sunday school is a good, dependable place to be.

The primary room may teach reverence. A place of beauty or worship will suggest quiet, joy, and peace. Pictures, flowers, an open Bible, or a lovely hanging will help focus the attention of the children.

The Ideal Primary Room

If the chairman of the Board of Christian Education or church school superintendent came to you and said, "You may have whatever you want in the way of rooms, materials, and equipment for your primary children," what would you ask for? Before we replied, many of us probably would think, "I ought to tell what I want immediately, before he changes his mind or spends the money for something else." Then we would begin to mention pictures, chairs, even the room on the other side of the building (the one in which the Women's Class meets) which we have wanted so long, and many other things.

When the Primary Department superintendent in a certain church school was asked that very question, she paused and said: "May I study and plan with my teachers about the needs of the children, evaluate what we already have, and discover what would contribute most to the growth of our children? Since we have the opportunity for this, we want our Primary Department to be as ideal as possible. We are deeply grateful to the church. May we meet with you later and explain our plans?"

Reading, conferences with decorators, visits to other church schools, consultation with parents, sketches and plans on paper, were all a part of the preparatory work of the primary leaders.

When they were ready the primary workers met with the Board of Christian Education and presented these plans for what they considered an ideal situation to meet the needs of their primary children. They explained:

"Primary children need light, warmth, and beauty. We would like our room to be on the first floor, with easy access to toilet

facilities and to the outdoors. One wall should be unbroken by windows and doors. The entrance door should be at the side or rear of the room. We want a room where the children may be seated without facing the light, preferably with it coming over their left shoulders. The room should be well ventilated and have clear-glass windows low enough for the children to see out. There should be provision for good artificial lighting on a dark day. There should be adequate heat so that the children will not have to wear outdoor garments.

"We know that primary children appreciate beauty of color, so the color scheme for our room is important. We know that the exposure of a room should be taken into consideration when planning the color scheme. A room with a great deal of sunlight on the south and east should be decorated in cool colors such as blues, grays, greens. A north and west room that is rather dark or gloomy should have warm colors such as tints of cream, yellow, buff, peach, or rose. Solid colors give a sense of distance and space. The ceiling should be lighter than the walls and the floors should be darker. When we know the size and location of our room, we will be ready to plan our color scheme.

"We would like to have rubber or asbestos tile or inlaid linoleum of a solid or two-tone color on the floor of our room. A rug will enhance its beauty. Large patterns or many figures in the floor covering are confusing. Whatever is chosen will be in harmony with the color scheme.

"A dado of cork or wallboard, two or three feet wide and placed around the walls of the room thirty inches from the floor, will provide a place for pictures, posters, and seasonal decorations. At the bottom of the dado should be a grooved picture rail, narrow ledge or shelf on which the children can stand their pictures.

"Our children will need a place for their wraps. The ideal arrangement would be a separate cloakroom, or low hooks in a corridor just outside our room. Above the hooks we would like a shelf for hats and below the hooks a shelf for galoshes. Otherwise, we can use a movable rack that can be screened off from the rest of the room, or hooks in some inconspicuous place on an inside wall.

"Primary children need space. They need space so they can move about freely, carry out the enterprises which they have planned,

and put into practice some of the skills in Christian living about which they have talked.

"We want a room that is large enough to provide for this activity and freedom of expression. Primary rooms should have eighteen square feet of space per child. A large assembly room and space for each class is desirable. Some primary teachers prefer separate classrooms, if adequate space is available.

"If we have a large room, separate class space may be arranged by the use of movable screens. A piece of wallboard about five feet square, framed with one-half inch wood about two inches wide and mounted on triangular stands, makes a usable screen. Casters will be placed in the standards so that the screen may be moved easily. If a larger screen is desired, wallboard or plywood four and one-half feet by eight feet, framed in wood three inches wide, may be used. One section of the screen may be equipped with a blackboard if desired. The screens should be painted to harmonize with the color scheme.

"Primary children need to be comfortable. They are growing and constantly active, and so they need equipment that will provide for ease, freedom, and comfort of movement. We want sturdy, light-weight, good posture chairs that can be moved easily by the children. The average height of the chairs should be fourteen inches. A few twelve-inch and sixteen-inch chairs would be desirable for the smaller and taller children. We would like to have rubber or metal gliders on the legs of the chairs.

"We want a rectangular-shaped table for each class. The top of the table should be approximately thirty inches by forty-eight to fifty-four inches and should stand ten inches higher than the chair seats. The chairs and tables should match in wood and finish. Several smaller tables will be needed for the interest centers.

"Our children will need low shelves on which they can arrange and keep their books, objects, and materials. We would like to have these in four-foot units that we can move easily and arrange in a variety of ways.

"Primary children need materials for worship. For the worship center we will want a low table, an attractive department Bible in large print and dark red, blue, or green binding. Our offering plates should be smaller, but similar to those used in the church worship service.

"We would like to have a few permanent pictures in our room. We want those that will speak a message to the children and also enhance the beauty of the room. One or two pictures from this list would be suitable:

Christ and the Children, Bella Vichon (Cizek School)
Follow Me, Tom Curr
The Arrival of the Shepherds, Lerolle
The Madonna of the Chair, Raphael
The Workshop at Nazareth, Briggs
Madonna and Child, Murillo
He Prayeth Best, Margaret Tarrant
Suffer the Little Children, Margaret Tarrant
The Angelus, Millet
The Sistine Madonna, Raphael (detail)

"*Primary children need to achieve.* A sense of achievement comes from doing things for oneself, and carrying enterprises through to satisfying results. Our children will need materials with which to work. Books for the reading center chosen because of their relationship to a particular unit of study will provide resource material and pleasure for the children. Construction paper, scissors, crayons, and the like will be needed for creative work and other activities.

"*The leaders of primary children will need:*
1. Primary graded lesson materials, including pupils' books, picture sets, teachers' textbooks, pamphlets for parents, and activity packets for the children.
2. Resource books and magazines for the teachers.
3. A cupboard for teachers' resource materials and supplies.
4. A place for each teacher to keep her wraps and purse.
5. A piano of good quality and in tune at all times.
6. A table for the secretary's use.
7. A picture file, placed and arranged for the use of both children and teachers.
8. Hymnbook: *Hymns for Primary Worship;* at least two copies, one for the pianist and another for the leader.

"We are deeply appreciative of your consideration and cooperation. We have planned with the ideal in mind. We realize that these plans are something toward which we, the teachers, the Board of Christian Education, the parents, in fact the entire church fellowship, will need to work."

It is not strange that the ideal place to meet was reached in three years in that church school. Careful study and planning, a growing interest and concern for primary children based on a knowledge of their needs (the Women's Bible Class offered to give up their room), and the co-operation of the entire church fellowship brought it to pass.

Grouping for Teaching

The following plans will suggest possible ways of grouping primary children for teaching:

For the Small Church

Plan 1. One primary class for children six, seven, and eight years of age.

Plan 2. Nursery—Children under four years of age.
Younger Children—Children four through seven years of age.
Older Children—Children eight through eleven years of age.

For the Medium-sized Church

Plan 1. Primary Department for children in grades 1, 2, and 3 (six, seven, and eight years of age), meeting together for worship and having separate class space for each age group.

Plan 2. Two-Grade Plan.
Primary Department—Children in grades 1 and 2 (six and seven years of age).
Primary-Junior or Lower Junior Department—Children in grades 3 and 4 (eight and nine years of age).
Junior Department—Children in grades 5 and 6 (ten and eleven years of age).
Under this plan each group is a department within itself and should have a room of its own. Some denominations now publish lesson materials for churches using this two-grade plan.

For a Large Church

Plan 1. Primary Department—Children in grades 1, 2, and 3 (six, seven, and eight years of age), meeting together for worship and having two or more classes for each grade or age.

Plan 2. Single Grade Plan.

    Primary Department I or Grade 1—Children six years of age.
    Primary Department II or Grade 2—Children seven years of age.
    Primary Department III or Grade 3—Children eight years of age.
    Each of these departments would meet by itself for the entire session. This plan would require three large rooms, one for each department.

In the Small Church

In one small church the primary class met in a corner to the right of the pulpit. A movable screen and the back of the piano formed two sides of the space and the two walls the other two sides. The back of the piano was draped with apple-green material. A picture on a low table with an open Bible placed before it formed a place of beauty. The screen was used for pictures, the children's drawings, and other work. Two orange crates, carefully sandpapered and painted ivory, served as shelves for books and work materials. Growing plants or bowls of flowers were always on the window sills. A table and chairs were the other equipment.

In another small church space was provided for the primary children in the rear corner of the room. One pew was placed against the back wall, another along the side wall. A movable screen was placed along the aisle. A piece of wallboard, attractively painted, was hung from the back of the pew which formed the fourth side of the class space. To this and the screen, pictures and other materials could be fastened. Three sections of a sectional bookcase served as a cupboard for the supplies. During the story or discussion the children sat on the pews. Large wooden blocks, painted a dark oak, served as footrests for the children. For certain types of activities, such as drawing, the children covered the pews with newspapers and used them as tables. The blocks of wood then served as seats.

The primary teacher in another small church turned the last two pews on one side of the room so that they faced each other with adequate space between them for her class activities. Orange crates were made into seats and the children faced toward the center for conversation and such, or turned toward the pews which they used for tables for activities. A cupboard made of orange crates and a low table by the teacher's chair were the only other pieces of equipment.

Lapboards, or shelves hinged to the back of the pews and dropped down when not in use will serve as worktables when the primary children have to meet in the pews for their class. Footrests that can be pushed under the pews when not in use should be provided for the comfort of the children.

Another primary teacher made a corner in the rear of the sanctuary attractive with a rug, a lovely worship center, chairs for the children, a dado on one wall, and attractive draperies at the one window. There was not room for a table. She enlisted the help of some junior high boys who cut, sandpapered, stained and varnished a piece of plywood, eighteen inches square, for each child. When the children needed a working surface, they turned their chairs to the wall, rested one edge of the wood on their knees and the opposite edge against the wall.

Small rooms on either side of the pulpit sometimes will provide excellent class space for primary children. Or a room in a near-by home may be used as the place of meeting.

In a two-room church where all the children's groups must use the same room, movable screens may be used to provide separate class spaces. In one such church, a new gas furnace had been installed. The coalbin, one corner partitioned off, was to be removed. The primary teacher asked that the bin be left in. It was thoroughly scrubbed and painted inside and out. Attractive curtains were hung at the high windows, a rug placed on the floor and wallboard was placed low on the walls for pictures. Low shelves for books and other materials were built in along the walls, and the room was provided with suitable chairs and a table. Thus, the "useless" coalbin was transformed into a most attractive and useful room for the primary children of that church school.

Arranging the Room

The purpose of equipment and its use is to provide for the comfort and well-being of primary children, to help them learn, and to provide an environment in which they can explore and carry out worth-while activities that contribute to their Christian growth. The more flexible the arrangement, the more usable the room will be. The arrangement of the equipment will depend upon the number of children, the size and shape of the room, and the

purpose of the session. The arrangement will vary from time to time as new purposes and work are undertaken.

Chairs arranged in a semicircle or hollow square encourage fellowship, sharing of experiences, and informality of procedure, and make an excellent arrangement for conference or planning periods with the children. If the shape and size of the room or the large number of children does not permit this arrangement, the chairs may be arranged in semicircular rows. The teacher's chair will always be within the group arrangement.

The library corner and book shelves should be placed where the light is adequate for reading.

Real flowers, growing plants, and vines should be cared for by the children, so vases and other containers will be placed on low shelves within easy reach.

The permanent pictures of the department will be framed simply and in harmony with the color scheme of the room. A few pictures will add beauty and help the children learn. Too many pictures are confusing and give a cluttered appearance to the room. Pictures should be hung on the eye level of the children. They should be hung on picture hooks with all cord and wire concealed by the picture. Large pictures should be hung on a large wall space. Smaller pictures may be grouped on a large wall space or hung separately on a smaller space.

Window shades, Venetian blinds, curtains, and draperies add to the homelikeness and beauty of the room if they are in harmony with the color scheme. They must be neatly and correctly hung and kept clean at all times. Window shades may be needed to soften glaring or too bright light. Heavy duplex shades, dark color on the outside and white or ivory on the inside, are excellent and are essential if the room is to be darkened for the use of projected visual material.

The interest centers or inviting corners for self-chosen activities will be placed where they will serve their purpose most effectively. Nature centers should be near windows. An exhibit table for objects from other lands might be near the dado on which related pictures could be placed. Tables for creative drawing, clay modeling or finger painting should be near the supply shelves. A wastebasket will be needed near the work center.

For worship the chairs may be arranged in a semicircle facing a wall space or a hanging in front of which the worship center has been arranged. The primary superintendent's chair should be placed to one side and not directly in front of the worship center. The piano will be near, but to one side of the worship center. The children should not face the light or the entrance door of the room. A blackboard should not be a part of the worship center. If there is a blackboard on the wall, velvet, monk's cloth or some other durable and attractive material of solid color in harmony with the color scheme may be hung from the top of the board to the floor so that it falls in soft folds. This will cover an unattractive object and provide a lovely wall hanging as a background for the worship center.

Let Us Begin Right Now

There are many things which we can do to make our rooms more attractive for children and a better place in which to teach.

Perhaps we need to begin with a good housecleaning! Wash the windows and woodwork, launder the curtains, thoroughly clean the walls, floors, rugs, and furniture. For some of us this will mean planning and co-operating with the janitor. For those of us who work in churches where there is no full-time janitor, it may mean hard work, but it will pay rich dividends in the experiences of the children and the satisfaction that comes to us in teaching in a clean place.

As we have cleaned and scrubbed, we may have discovered that the paint on the walls, woodwork or furniture is worn, knocked off in spots or can no longer be made attractive with just soap and water. New paint is what is needed. If the budget of the church does not allow for the services of a professional decorator, almost any church will buy paint if there is someone to do the work. As long as we are redecorating, we shall want to make the room as inviting and beautiful as possible, so we will plan carefully for the color scheme. Then we may enlist the co-operation of the parents of our children in the work of painting. A simple meal together and then work, or work followed by light refreshments will provide opportunities for fellowship, sharing of common interests, and a growing understanding, as well as getting the painting done. Or the help of the young people in the church may be enlisted. Sometimes they are just waiting for an opportunity to be of service. Such a project can be for them an experience in Christian service.

What else can we do to improve the general appearance of the room? Look at that piano! It is anything but orderly. How did these old candles, odds and ends of paper, hymnbooks, handkerchiefs, empty vases, two children's purses, and a boy's cap happen to be there anyway? Off they must come. We will leave nothing on the top and only the primary hymnbook, *Hymns for Primary Worship,* on the front of it. There, that looks much better. If the children bring some short-stemmed flowers next Sunday, they may wish to place a low bowl of them on the top of the piano, or they may wish to place the low bowl of ivy near the end so that the vine trails over the side. But let us, the teachers, observe the unwritten sign that reads, "No teachers' hats or purses here—not even those of the pianist."

Let us survey the room next for "excess baggage." We will keep only those things which are needed to help children grow in Christian ways and which relate to the present unit of study. That wall frieze over there ought to come down. The children made that last summer. It has served its purpose. It really should have been taken down a long time ago. And that model of a Palestinian village—when did the children make it? It certainly is dilapidated and dirty.

Those stacks of story papers on the secretary's desk—yes, they have been accumulating from week to week. Let us sort them and put them away in the supply cupboard. No wonder they are on the table. The secretary probably couldn't get them into the cupboard! It has been the "catch-all" for everything that we didn't know what to do with. Cleaning the cupboard means washing and cleaning the shelves, discarding unneeded objects and materials, sorting and arranging teaching materials by quarters and years, arranging the resource materials for the teachers, such as magazines and books, so that they can be easily located, cleaning and placing the flower containers ready for use, sorting and arranging all other materials in neat stacks or labeled boxes, putting away seasonal material. There, now that that is done, we have room in the cupboard. How nice it looks! The children will learn something about orderliness and the care of materials when they see this.

Now let us see about the pictures. Looks as if we kept adding pictures without taking any down. Our next unit of study is on "Jesus and the Children." We will move this beautiful picture, *Suffer the Little Children,* by Margaret Tarrant, from the side wall to the worship center. We will take all the other pictures down and place them in the picture file.

We have discovered that we need to go through the picture file, sorting, mending, cleaning, and remounting some pictures. There are some that must be discarded. While we are doing this, we will check our pictures with those listed in the graded lesson picture sets to see that our file is complete. We will order those sets which are incomplete.

Next we must turn our attention to the chairs and furnishings.

If a piece of equipment cannot be satisfactorily or attractively repaired, we will discard it. Furniture polish, stain, or paint will improve the appearance of most furniture.

Now, let us study the arrangement of our room. Perhaps we can use our space to much better advantage by relocating the class groups. If we have not had a worship center, we will plan one. Perhaps we need to arrange a library corner with a table near the low shelves on which some children's books may be placed. Our next study is a missionary unit. The children will enjoy reading books and looking at pictures about children in another land.

Primary Children May Help Too

Since this is the children's room, they should have a part in the planning and work. There are many things which they can do. Cleaning and caring for their low shelves and supplies will help them grow in responsibility. Arranging and caring for flowers, bulbs, and plants will help them grow in appreciation of beauty and God's laws concerning it. Choosing the materials and arranging the worship center will help them learn about worship and reverence. A low bulletin board with a list on it of the things to be done each Sunday morning will serve as a source of guidance for the children.

FOR FURTHER STUDY

1. What is there in your Primary Department room or equipment that aids or hinders worth-while experiences of fellowship, work, and worship with the children? What do you need to discard? What do you need to add?

2. Draw a room plan taking into consideration the number of primary children in your department and your type of grouping. Arrange the equipment for worship and work.

3. What improvements can you make with little cost? What immediate steps can and will you take to make these improvements a reality?

4. What do your primary children learn from their room? Does this contribute to or hinder their Christian growth?

CHAPTER 4

Using Lesson Materials

DANIEL WEBSTER said, "If we work upon marble, it will perish; if upon brass, time will efface it; if we rear temples, they will crumble into dust, but if we work upon immortal minds, if we imbue them with the principles of righteousness, with the just fear of God and love of our fellow man, we engrave on those tablets something which will brighten through all eternity."

A good workman needs the finest tools available for his work. He also needs to know how to use them. So it becomes imperative for every primary teacher to have the best lesson materials available and to know how to use them skillfully, if she would guide children in Christian living.

What Are Primary Graded Courses?

Primary graded courses are planned for use with children who are six, seven, and eight years of age or in the first, second, and third grades of the public school. These courses have been written by people who have had experience with these children and who know best what Bible material and ways of teaching will meet the needs of the children, and achieve our objectives for Christian education. The primary graded courses are part of a whole series prepared for use with persons from the Nursery through the Senior High departments. These graded courses put out by the various denominations provide for a progressive development and a well-rounded program of Christian education for growing persons.

The Bible

The essential source book for all our church school teaching is the Bible. At the heart of every teaching unit and every session within that unit is carefully selected Bible material which is suitable for primary children.

We may have thought that telling a Bible story and teaching a Bible verse was the only way to use biblical material with primary children. There are many meaningful ways for primary teachers and children to use the Bible together.

Bible truths and principles are not an end in themselves, but are guides for living. Since the child learns through doing, his active participation is essential. We should provide many opportunities for him to try out great Bible principles in daily living. For example, a Bible story may be told in one session. Then for several sessions following, other materials, both biblical and nonbiblical, may be used to help him discover how the truth in the Bible story works out in daily living and to create in him a desire to follow it in his own life. It is wise to move slowly and to help the child to see and live the Bible principle in many situations and relationships.

The Bible is essentially an adult book. Not all of the Bible material is suitable for use with primary children. We use some of it over and over again with them, in new relationships and a variety of ways. Primary children are confused when too much Bible material is used, and particularly if it is difficult to understand. Bible material must be suited to their needs and ability to understand.

Graded lessons for primary children include a wide range of Bible material to be used in many ways. The material is chosen carefully so that it may make the greatest contribution to the child's growth at this particular age. Graded courses provide many opportunities for these children to appreciate and live according to Bible principles. The primary child will also find that the Bible verses in the primary graded lessons give him a language for worship.

The Bible itself should have a place of honor in every Primary Department and class. A beautifully bound Bible should be used in the worship center. Occasionally the older children may read single verses or simple passages from it. A Bible printed in clear, large type with the lines running all the way across the page is much more suitable for use with primary children than one printed in fine type in two columns.

When the teacher or superintendent tells a Bible story, she should let the children know that it is a Bible story. She should have a Bible in her hand or near by so that she may show where the story is found. If it is a story that might have happened in Bible times, such as some of the stories of the boyhood of Jesus, the teacher may say, "I do not find this story in my Bible, but because we know how people lived and what they did in Bible times, this is a story that might have happened."

Carefully chosen Bible-story books suited to the age of the children, and having good illustrations, may be used on the library table or may be read to the children in informal periods.

The teacher's own attitude and her use of the Bible with the children helps their love and appreciation for the Book to grow. The teacher will have her Bible with her at every class session. In the graded courses the Old Testament references are taken from the American Standard Version and the New Testament references from the Revised Standard Version. After 1952 all Bible references will be taken from the Revised Standard Version. The children know without the teacher speaking of it how much she loves the Bible. Unless her appreciation of the Bible is sincere and unless she has some knowledge of its teachings, she cannot help the children to develop in their appreciation and understanding of it as they should. As the children see and know that their teacher reads and follows the teachings of the Bible, they are challenged to know and follow its teachings, too.

The Teacher's Book

The teacher's book, or quarterly as it is sometimes called, gives the teacher complete and specific guidance for the class session. The teacher's book is a source book of suggested plans, materials, and procedures. The Bible material is an essential part of all these materials and plans. There are also suggestions for moments of informal worship, varied activities, conversation about ways of living, stories, pictures, music, and the like. Detailed teaching plans for each session are given. These will be especially helpful to the less experienced teacher. A faithful week-by-week study and planning with the help of the teacher's book is one of the best ways of learning how to teach. On the other hand, the more experienced teacher will know how to use her teacher's book as a guide to help her make her own teaching plans.

Pupils' Books

Realizing the great need for a closer co-operation with the home in the Christian nurture of primary children, a number of denominations are now publishing books for pupils' use at home. These are published quarterly and take the place of the pupils' lesson leaflets. They are reading books which are of interest to the child, and for this reason of interest also to his parents. These books are beautifully illustrated and contain Bible stories, verses, songs, poems, and suggestions for home activities. At the completion of his three years in the Primary Department, the child will have a library of reading books of Bible stories and other helpful materials. The material in the pupil's book is related to the class sessions, and guidance for the use of it is given in the teacher's book. The teacher will need a copy for class use.

Other denominations provide lesson leaflets or papers, each of which contains a picture, Bible verse, story, poem, or other material. These are related to the class session and the child may take the lesson leaflet home each Sunday.

Activity Materials

There may be quarterly activity materials which are a part of the courses of study. These usually consist of envelopes which contain a variety of work materials. They are planned for individual use, so each child and teacher will need a set. The teacher is given help in her teacher's book on the best ways to use each activity sheet.

Story Papers

Primary children need interesting, wholesome reading material which is graded for their reading ability and interests. Most denominations prepare a weekly story paper for primary children. These primary papers contain stories, devotional thoughts, simple patterns for activities, pictures, and other types of materials, all of which have value for their growth in Christian thoughts, attitudes, and actions.

Selecting and Using Other Materials

There are other materials which will enrich the children's experiences and help them learn, if wisely selected and used. Concerning any material, the teacher will do well to ask herself: "How will this material influence the thinking, feeling, and behavior of my children and contribute to the realization of my purpose? Will I have to leave out something better to have time to use this?"

Messages to Parents

In addition to the suggestions for parents that are given in the pupils' books, most denominations publish a special quarterly folder for the parents. This is a special message to the parents. It tells briefly what the children will be studying in the church school and contains many suggestions of ways in which the parents may carry on these Christian purposes with their children in the home. The teacher may take this folder with her when she visits each home at the beginning of each quarter. She should try her best to help the parents feel that it is a personal message to them.

Pictures

Pictures are silent teachers. They stir the primary child's imagination and stimulate his actions. They bring stories to life. Through pictures the child learns of customs, manners, and peoples of Bible times and other lands. They create an atmosphere, suggest attitudes and ways of prayer and worship to the primary child. Pictures help to make religious truths vivid and vital.

1. *In selecting pictures* for use with primary children we will be guided by their needs and interests. Children like pictures in which there are persons, preferably children, who are doing something. Landscapes and historic pictures have little appeal. Detailed pictures of flowers, birds, and such may be used when the objects themselves are not available. Pictures should be simple in detail. Too many characters or details in a picture confuse children. Pictures should have good coloring, clear printing, and be accurate in information and adequate in concepts.

Many are familiar with the picture of the two children gathering flowers at the edge of the cliff with a guardian angel near by. The concept is that God's love and care expressed through the angel will protect the children, and, regardless of what they do, the children will not fall over the cliff. Such a picture is not suitable for use with children for three reasons. First, there is symbolism in it and primary children do not understand symbolism. Second, it conveys a half truth that might lead to danger for children. God does love and care for children, but he expects them to work with him in caring for themselves. Third, the picture is not considered good art.

2. There are many ways of *using pictures* in teaching primary children. A picture may be used to create an atmosphere of worship, as well as in the worship itself. A unit of study may be introduced with pictures. They may be used as resource material to which the children will go for information. Pictures may be used to stimulate conversation. Pictures may be used after a story to make vivid the characters, events, or customs. If there is something in the story which is unfamiliar to the children, a picture may sometimes be used before the story is told. Pictures may be used for recall and review and to teach new songs.

3. *The sources* of pictures are numerous. The picture sets which accompany most graded courses of study provide an excellent source of pictures. There are usually eight to twelve pictures in the set for each quarter and each picture is related to a class session. The pictures have been carefully selected for primary children. Copies of many of the masterpieces of art are included in these sets.

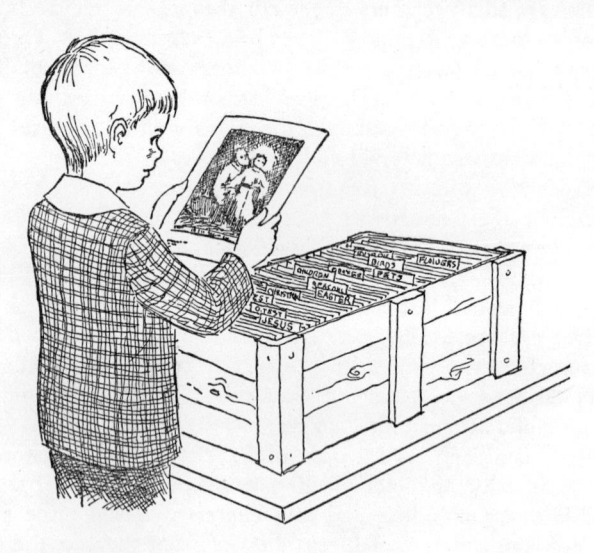

Many denominational publishing houses also carry in various sizes copies of some of the masterpieces and other pictures which are valuable for teaching. These will be listed in their catalogue.

Occasionally a picture on a calendar or in a magazine will be suitable.

4. *Filing and caring for pictures* is important. All pictures printed on lightweight paper should be neatly cut and mounted on cardboard. Large drawers in the supply cupboard may serve as a file for pictures; or a large box, attractively painted, may be kept in an accessible place for both children and teachers. Pictures should be grouped according to the subjects with which they will be most useful. For example, they may be classified according to the persons represented, the season, the stories, the character traits portrayed, the Old and the New Testament.

Music and Songs

Primary children like to sing. Music provides a language of worship for them and helps them grow in appreciation of the beautiful. They express their feeling of joy and thankfulness to God in their songs. Singing together creates a sense of fellowship, and a primary child may express his joy in sharing and co-operation with other children through a song. A six-year-old broke into song during a work period. "Friends, Friends, Friends," he sang. Then he smiled at the teacher and said, "It's fun to make things with them." The song had been the spontaneous outward expression of his inner thoughts and feelings. Instrumental music and songs help to develop and fulfill the purposes of the units of study. Music composed by peoples of other lands and races can help the child grow in his appreciation of the contribution which many people have made to the happiness of others, and to him.

1. *Selecting Songs.* We select songs carefully for they are teaching aids. Not all songs are suitable for primary children. The teacher has the responsibility for selecting from many sources those songs which will help children to live in most worth-while ways now. The primary child lives in the present, not in the past or the future, and his experiences in singing should be related to everyday experiences, and meet his religious needs. The concepts of the songs should be Christian and express the child's ideas and feelings

Songs should be short and words easily understood. If a teacher has to spend much time in explanation, the song is not suitable.

The melody should be within range of the children's voices, preferably on the musical staff. The mood of the music should uphold the meaning of the words.

2. *Using Songs.* We will use songs with primary children when there is a need and readiness for them. A class of primary children stood in awe and wonder at the edge of a pond which was surrounded by trees, bordered by flowers, and covered with water lilies. It was a beautiful place. One of the children said, "I feel like singing, but I don't know what to sing." The children sat down at the edge of the pond, and in a short time had learned the song, "All Things Bright and Beautiful." They might have created their own song.

Songs give the child a language of worship, but we should not teach a new song during the time of worship. A song may be learned as part of a class experience. It may be related to and used with a picture. A song may be used to recall or describe a story or a happy experience, or just for fun and fellowship.

The entire song should be introduced at one time in order that the children may know the complete thought of the song. The teacher may use it as a poem or sing it softly to the children. They will listen to the melody. The teacher will sing it again while the children hum the melody. They are then ready to sing.

Many of the songs the teacher will use will be listed in the teacher's book. Most of these songs will be found either in the pupil's book or in the primary hymnal, *Hymns for Primary Worship.* Some teachers build up a valuable collection of songs for primary children in a loose-leaf notebook. Songs may be clipped from denominational magazines for leaders, teachers' books, children's folders or books, and story papers.

3. *Listening Music.* As primary children listen to beautiful music, desirable emotions may be aroused, thinking may be stimulated, and appreciation developed. (Listening to music develops powers of concentration and self-control in the children.) Descriptive, instrumental music may help the children to think and evaluate, and may lead to expression through some activity. At the close of a class when some first-grade children had been listening to a record to hear the songs of birds, the ripple of the brook, and the wind in the trees, one of the children said, "I was listening so close I wasn't saying a word."

In churches where each class has its own room, or occasionally when music on a piano or record-player will not disturb other groups, the teacher will find that instrumental music, so employed, will afford a worth-while experience for the children.

Stories

A story is only one of the many tools which a teacher will use to help her boys and girls grow in Christian ways. It is no longer regarded as the most essential part of a session. Stories may be used to help children solve a problem, to give information, to motivate a unit of study, to create sympathetic understanding of people of other lands, to recall experiences, to develop appreciation, and as a guide for worship. They may occasionally be used for fun and fellowship.

Stories must be carefully selected to meet the immediate needs and interests of the children and be within their ability to understand. They should be closely related to the purposes of the session, set forth the highest and best principles of Christian living, and make a definite contribution to the child's religious growth.

Graded lesson materials, denominational magazines, children's story papers, vacation church school units, and missionary books are all good sources of stories. Books of stories, such as *The Story Shop* and *Another Story Shop,* by Mary C. Odell, are also excellent.

A teacher will find it helpful to develop a story file of her own. One teacher found the following divisions of her story file most helpful: seasonal stories, Old Testament, New Testament, missionary, special days, and character traits (honesty, courtesy, kindness to animals, friendship, sharing and taking turns, and co-operation).

Poems

Poems suitable for the primary child help him express his feelings and thoughts. Through poems the child may give expression to unbounded happiness and love of beauty. They help create an attitude of worship and provide the child with a language with which to express his feelings of worship. They stimulate wonder and awe or stir imagination. They vivify experience for him. They provide moments of appreciation of the beautiful and lead to a further search for that which is beautiful. A child has a sense of belonging to a group as he listens to and enjoys poems with it. Poems may appeal to the child's interest in rhythm and imitation.

They may be used with primary children for pure enjoyment. Poetry speaks to the feelings rather than to the intellect.

The graded lesson materials, children's papers and books, and leaders' magazines contain many excellent poems for use with the children. Memorize them and use them. Make the poem live for the children as you enter into its mood, rhythm, and feeling. If it is a "fun" poem, enjoy it and laugh with the children. The words of a song may be used as a poem. Many Bible passages are poetic in form and feeling, and will have added value when they are used as poetry. A copy of the Bible in which the poetic literature is printed in poetic form will be helpful to the teacher.

There should be books of poetry in every Primary Department for the use of the teachers and children. These are excellent:

Silver Pennies, B. J. Thompson
More Silver Pennies, B. J. Thompson
Secrets, Jessie O. Jones

Children may create and write their own poems, individually or in groups. The creation of poetry grows out of a vital experience or because the children see and feel the need for a poem to use. A class of primary children had been learning a song which they were to share with some children who were coming to visit their class. The song was a friendship song, and very appropriate.

"Do you suppose that we could write another verse for our song that would tell the children that being friendly is God's way for all children?" the teacher asked.

"Why don't we just say that Bible verse, 'A friend loveth at all times'?" Elaine suggested.

"Perhaps we could use that verse in the stanza of our song. Shall we try?" the teacher suggested.

Soon the children had created a third stanza for the song, using the Bible verse in it. There was a felt need and the creation of the poem grew out of this. The teacher will find in her teacher's book help in using this method of teaching.

Audio-Visual Materials

Pictures, objects, trips to places, and models bring concrete visual experience to the child. Children learn through seeing. Visual materials may be projected or nonprojected.

1. *Nonprojected Materials.* Study and work with nature specimens, such as cocoons, flowers, birds' nests, pine cones, and sea shells may provide many learning experiences for the children and lead to a growing appreciation of God, the Creator. Firsthand experiences with these are of more value than pictures or conversation about them. We remember best those things which we see and touch.

Objects, costumes, and curios from other lands help the children learn of the manners and customs of the people. Many missionary and sharing enterprises have grown out of the wise use of such objects with children.

Models of Palestinian houses, Oriental lamps, scrolls, and the like help the children visualize Bible customs and modes of living and provide a background of understanding for their Bible stories and verses.

2. *Projected Materials.* Many churches have or soon will have projectors for showing slides, filmstrips, or motion pictures. Some will have also opaque projectors for showing pictures, children's drawings, and other flat objects.

Slides, motion pictures, or filmstrips which are used with primary children should be clear and with no unnecessary details. The main characters or objects should stand out distinctly. The quality of the art work should be authentic and good. They should be accurate in their portrayal of events, customs, or peoples. They should be appropriate for primary children as to content and length. They should be related to the other teaching materials and activities. The teacher should be thoroughly familiar with whatever she plans to use. She should prepare the children for what they are to see. There will be conversation following the use of the material. In some cases it might be well to show the films, filmstrips, or slides a second time.

An opaque projector, or reflectoscope, is valuable in teaching primary children because it may be used to project on the screen, so that all may see, their own drawings, pictures in their reading books, or other similar materials.

3. *Records.* Each Primary Department should have a record player, if possible. Many excellent records for children are being produced by denominational houses and commercial firms. Records may be used for listening music wherever the situation allows.

Some story records are excellent. Primary children may make their own records in class. The same principles of selection and use apply to records as to other teaching aids.

Most denominations have prepared lists of audio-visual resources for use with their graded lesson materials for children. Write to your denomination for such a list. Other sources are listed in the teachers' books.

Getting Ready to Teach

Materials (both courses of study and resource materials) are important, but more important is the way in which the teacher uses them in the class session. Materials may have value in themselves for the growth of children, but if they are not used wisely, they may lose all or much of their value. At the center of the teacher's planning is the child, each child in her class. His needs, interests, and abilities are the basis of her plans, whatever materials she may use. She repeatedly asks herself, "How will these materials and the way I use them affect the thinking, feeling, and actions of my children? What knowledge will my children acquire? What attitudes will be developed? What skills in Christian living will be practiced?"

Many times teachers are not willing to pay the price of successful teaching in careful planning and thorough preparation. A teacher cannot pick up a quarterly on Saturday night, read the session through hurriedly, and expect to guide children effectively on Sunday morning.

1. *Studying the Teacher's Book.* When you are given a new teacher's book at the beginning of a quarter, first open your book and read through the Table of Contents and the general Introduction. These first few pages are very important and contain material that will be helpful to a teacher. Sometimes teachers skip over this material and then wonder why they do not know what to do. If you are using a primary graded course, your quarterly will be divided not into thirteen separate lessons, but into two or three units. Read also the introduction to each unit, studying especially its purpose. Note that this purpose is definitely related to one or more of the general objectives for the Christian education of children described in chapter 2. See how one unit leads naturally to the next one. Picture for yourself how you may expect

your children to grow in Christian living during these next three months.

2. *What Is a Unit?* A unit is a series of worth-while experiences bound together around some center of child interest and need. All the materials and activities in each session of a unit are closely related and make their contribution to the general purpose of the unit. Most units in the primary graded courses are short, running only four or five weeks. The order of units in a course has been determined sometimes by seasonal interest, as in the case of the Christmas and Easter units, sometimes so as to provide a balanced program of Christian education for the three years a child is in the Primary Department.

3. *Preparing for a Unit.* As stated above, read carefully the introduction to the unit and the purpose for each session. Make sure that you understand the reason for this study. Read the suggestions given for planning and carrying out the unit. You will find the unit outline chart very helpful. Consider whether you will need to adapt it slightly in order better to meet your own children's experiences and needs. Check the activities that you think would be most practicable for your children and that would contribute most to their Christian growth. Do not try to use them all. Remember that every unit is planned to give a wide choice of activities to teachers in different teaching situations. Read the Bible material carefully and try to understand why these passages are suitable for primary children and will help to achieve your purpose. Make a note of other materials you will need for the activities you have chosen. Then, and not until then, are you really ready to start preparing to teach the first session.

4. *Preparing to Teach a Session.* Perhaps you are preparing to teach a session called "A Friend to the Unfriendly." This is a part of a five-week unit on "Stories of Jesus." The following suggestions may help you in your preparation:

a. Spend time in prayer and meditation for your children, your own needs, and God's guidance as you teach.

b. Recall the experiences of the past two weeks as the children have thought about "Jesus, the Children's Friend" and "Jesus' Kindness to the Sick." Jot them down on paper for ready reference.

c. Study the purpose for this week's session and see how these new experiences are related to the earlier ones which you had noted.

d. Discover what Bible material is to be used. Read the comments about it given in the teacher's book. A Bible commentary will be helpful in studying the passage. Note how each reference is to be used. What part forms the story? What is to be memorized? Observe the brief verses to be read directly from the Bible to the children. Recall the verse that was used last week.

e. Read the suggested plans for the class session. Take time to consider the session plans in the light of the needs of each child. Decide whether the plans should be adapted in any way in order to be more helpful to your group. Visualize your classroom and equipment.

f. Think of the amount of time you have and the best possible use of it. If your teaching time is brief, pay special attention to the plans given for a short session. If you have a longer time, read over the plans given for a second hour or an expanded session. If you have both younger and older children in your group, note the special suggestions for one primary class.

g. Study the picture from the Picture Set and the Activity Sheet to be used during the session. Discover ways of using the pupil's book in class. Be sure you are thoroughly familiar with these materials.

h. Read the list of materials needed for this session. Check your session plan to make sure you have everything.

i. Study the suggestions of things to do as you get ready. Make sure they have all been done. Be sure you are prepared to tell the story and to lead a discussion which will make the children think.

j. Plan to arrive early, some time before the arrival of the first child. With your hat and coat off and out of sight, you are ready to greet the first child and start him on some activity of interest.

k. Write out your own session plan on paper. You may decide to follow the one given in your teacher's book, but it will help you to write out your own outline, including only those activities you will use. Remember, however, that you will want to be alert to recognize ideas which originate in your own class group and which may involve a sudden change in teaching plan.

When a teacher makes such careful preparation, she is ready to guide her children in worth-while experiences and exploration of great Bible truths and ways of Christian living.

"Do your best to present yourself to God as one approved, a workman who has no need to be ashamed, rightly handling the word of truth" (2 Tim. 2:15).

For Further Study

1. Think over the needs of your children. Study the lesson material you will use for next Sunday's session. How will this material meet the needs of your children?

2. What will the children learn from your attitude toward and appreciation of the Bible?

3. Study your lesson materials for the present quarter and discover in how many different ways the Bible material is used.

4. Investigate all materials which your denomination prepares for use with primary children. Are you using all of them? If not, which ones would you like to ask your primary superintendent to get for you? Why?

5. If you are not providing the story papers of your denomination for your primary children, order some samples for study and use with the children.

6. Plan and prepare a satisfactory picture file for your class or department.

7. Use the suggestions under "Getting Ready to Teach," as a guide in preparing your session plan for next Sunday.

CHAPTER 5
Ways of Teaching

A VISITOR entered a Primary Department one Sunday in November. She was greeted by the superintendent and made to feel welcome. She looked about the room. It was a large room on the southeast corner of the building. The walls were painted soft blue. The ceiling was tinted oyster white, and the woodwork was pearl gray. The hardwood floor was covered with a taupe rug. Venetian blinds and printed drapes in which rose shades predominated, softened the glare of the bright sunlight which streamed through clear, shining windows. Three beautiful pictures, *The Pilgrims Going to Church* by Boughton, *The Angelus* by Millet, and *Father, We Thank Thee* by Wireman, hung low on the walls. The room was a place of beauty. The visitor soon discovered that it was a place of action also.

As each primary child entered the room, he was welcomed by two children and a teacher who formed the welcoming committee. After he had hung his outdoor clothing in the cloakroom, he made his way to one of the interest centers or the bulletin board.

In one corner of the room near the book shelves was a library table on which books had been placed, invitingly open, for the children to explore.

In another part of the room a few nature specimens, a bird's nest, autumn leaves, and the like, had been arranged. On the table were a magnifying glass and a microscope for the children to use in examining the treasures.

A teacher was at the piano. The primary hymnal was open to the hymn, "For the Fruit upon the Tree." On a table near the piano were pictures which the children might choose to illustrate the song.

Crayons, scissors, white paper, and paints were ready for use on a worktable near the low shelves on which the children kept their supplies.

The "Bulletin Board," a piece of white paper thumbtacked to the dado, had these suggestions printed on it:

WE WILL BE THINKING ABOUT THE LOVING-KINDNESS OF THE LORD

THINGS TO DO THIS MORNING

1. Choose a picture for the worship center
2. Put autumn leaves around the dado
3. Find something interesting about the treasures on the nature table
4. Read a book and learn how God cares for us
5. Arrange the flowers in vases
6. Arrange the place of offering
7. Learn a new song
8. Draw or paint a picture to illustrate a Bible verse that tells us of the loving-kindness of the Lord

A teacher stayed near the bulletin board to assist any child who needed help in reading the suggestions, and to place the child's name after the thing he chose to do.

When most of the children had arrived, quiet music called them from the interest centers to their chairs, which were arranged in a semicircle. For a brief period of time they talked about the discoveries which they had made about God's loving-kindness. They were beginning a new unit of study called "The Loving-kindness of the Lord." Some of the drawings were shared. The group of children that had learned the song taught it to the others. A few of the nature treasures were talked about. The children then made suggestions of other things they would like to know, and of other things they might do to learn more about the loving-kindness of the Lord. The superintendent guided this sharing period so carefully that all that was done contributed to the development of the purposes of the unit and session.

At the close of the sharing period, the children went to their class groups. The first-grade children were learning about ways in which God cares for them. The second-grade children were discovering ways of helping to care for God's world, and the third-graders were learning of ways of worshiping God.

The visitor discovered that the teacher of the first-grade class began her class period with a discussion and study of the picture, *Jesus Teaching*. She told the Bible story of Jesus teaching about

God's care. After the story the children again enjoyed talking about the picture. They were then ready to listen to the Bible verse, Psalm 33:5, which the teacher read from her Bible. Prayer naturally followed. The children drew pictures of things that tell of God's care.

Quiet music called the children from their class groups to the place of worship. The picture, *He Prayeth Best*, by Margaret Tarrant, had been chosen and arranged in the worship center by the children. A bowl of flowers and an open Bible had been placed on the low table. The superintendent guided the children as they worshiped. All materials which she used were closely related to the theme, "The Loving-kindness of the Lord."

After the worship there was a brief conference period in which the children talked about the discoveries they were to try to make during the following week, the reading they were to do at home in their pupils' books, and the things which they were to bring next Sunday. A new child was welcomed and a birthday was remembered. Fifteen minutes for the sharing period, thirty minutes for the class time, ten minutes for worship, and five minutes for fellowship together at the close had filled the scheduled one-hour session. The session had really started when the first child had arrived, for those early happenings were related to and prepared the children for sharing, study, and work.

In this church most of the children remained for the second hour or expanded session while their parents were in the morning church service. Under the same adult leadership the children planned and carried through many activities that were not possible in a session of one hour. Many teacher's textbooks in the graded courses contain suggestions and materials for use in an expanded session.

On this particular morning the children took a walk outdoors to discover evidences of God's loving-kindness. Upon their return they talked about their discoveries. They learned and illustrated a song and listened to a story. In the closing moments of informal worship, they remembered some Bible verses, sang again the song which they had learned, and then prayed.

As the last child left, the visitor said to herself, "This has been a most worth-while morning for everyone—children, teachers, and me. How happy the children were! And the teachers seemed to find their teaching a joyous privilege. I wonder why?" To answer her questions she began to evaluate the session, thinking of what had happened to the children and the methods the teachers had used to accomplish their purposes.

What were the experiences of the morning which contributed to the Christian growth of the children? They had had *fellowship* together in sharing discoveries with one another, taking a walk, working in the interest centers, and learning a new song. They had *studied* together as they examined the nature treasures, listened to stories, learned Bible verses, and enjoyed pictures. They had learned through the *activities* in which they had participated. They had *worshiped.* The sharing period at the beginning of the session and the class experiences had prepared the children for meaningful worship. Children grow through fellowship, study, service activities, and worship. Careful planning and guidance by the teachers, and active participation of the children in planning and carrying the activities through, had made these experiences both meaningful and worth while.

What methods had the teachers used to provide such worthwhile experiences for the children? There had been conversation, picture study, memorizing a song and Bible verses, storytelling, drawing, investigating and examining nature treasures, reading, taking a walk, choosing pictures, carrying through chosen activities. All materials and methods were suitable for the age of the children and related to the purposes of the session and the unit. The teacher had been a guide. No wonder she came to the end of the morning with a warm glow of satisfaction! No wonder teaching was a privilege to her! She had worked with busy, happy children, and their reactions and responses brought satisfaction to her.

When the visitor walked from the church, she realized that she wanted to come back next Sunday. She knew that the children and their leaders were launched upon a study that would cover several weeks, and she was eager to see where it would lead.

Fellowship

Fellowship has been defined as friendly companionship. Fellowship provides opportunities for growing in relationships with other persons, and that is one of our general objectives in the Christian education of primary children.

As the children arrive, the informality of the early moments of the session offers time for friendly greetings and sharing interesting incidents of the past week. The children and their teachers, and many times parents and other members of the church family, will have a part. The teachers may make many meaningful contacts with the parents at this time.

Fellowship should characterize the entire session of the Primary Department. However, there are times of planned fellowship.

There will be a time of welcome for new boys and girls, or those who have been absent. An appropriate song, a Bible verse, and words of greeting will make this a happy occasion for them.

Birthdays will be remembered during the planned fellowship period. Sometimes a birthday card or other form of recognition is given to the "birthday" child. The songs, "Sing About a Birthday" or "Glad I Am to Grow," in *Hymns for Primary Worship,* will add to the joyousness of the occasion. A spoken or choral prayer, such as "Prayer on a Birthday," in the same hymnal, will give deep religious significance to the birthday.

The learning of new songs, Bible passages, or poems is a fellowship experience, for it is a friendly adventure together to understand the meaning and memorize the words. The learning of new worship materials should never be a part of the worship service itself. The new hymn or Bible passage may be learned during a fellowship period or in the class group, and used later in the worship service.

The sharing of reports, dramatizations, and pictures may be experiences of fellowship. Announcements should be made during the time of fellowship.

Play is an important part of the primary child's life. Much character development comes through play. Sometimes suggestions for games or play are made in the session plans in the teacher's book. If so, they are there for a purpose and will contribute to the child's Christian development. Brief periods may be devoted to rest and play during the morning session, particularly if it is an expanded period covering two hours. These are periods of fellowship. Occasional class and department parties will offer other opportunities for fun and fellowship. If a true spirit of fellowship is to be maintained during parties and play periods, all rivalry, exciting contests, games which divide rather than unify the group, and overstimulation will be avoided.

Excursions, trips to interesting places, nature walks, and picnics are also times of fellowship for children and teachers.

Worship

Worship is an experience of fellowship with God. Any situation which brings the child in close relationship with God may lead to moments of worship. These times may come in the presence of the beauties of nature, when studying a picture, as the climax of a conversation, or they may be stimulated by a song, poem, or Scripture passage. Often during the class session the activities will so stimulate the thinking and emotions of the child that worship is a natural outcome. Such experiences are spontaneous and natural, and grow out of the child's need to express himself. Alert teachers who are sensitive to the feelings of children will be quick to recognize and make the most of such opportunities for informal worship when they arise.

Planned worship services, simple but meaningful, provide opportunities for group participation in worship. These services will not take the place of informal worship. The planned service will be most helpful when it grows out of the other experiences of the class session. These services should be brief. Ten or fifteen minutes are adequate.

The environment for worship is important. Since most of us must use for worship the same room in which other activities are carried on, space at the side or front of the room may be set aside for worship and should be kept specifically for that purpose, if at all possible. A worship center which is attractive and meaningful will help to focus attention. We must not depend upon it as a substitute for the experience of worship. It is not an end, but a means to an end. Its meaning and use will need to be interpreted and made evident to the children. The children will help plan for and arrange the worship center. It will be changed from time to time according to the theme of the service or seasonal interest. A low table, an appropriate picture, an open Bible, a vase of flowers, or a growing plant help to create beauty. Artificial flowers are not appropriate for use in a worship center. If a wall hanging is used for a background, it should be good in quality, harmonious in color with the rest of the room decorations, and contribute to the beauty of the worship center.

All the other persons in the room are a part of the child's environment for worship. Teachers will sit with their children and participate in the service. Such distractions as are caused by adults—getting out equipment, counting money, ringing bells, drills, calls for loud singing, announcements, or reports—must be eliminated. This calls for tactful and prayerful co-operation on the part of all.

Providing the primary child with a language of worship is essential. He needs training in attitudes of worship. He needs to know materials through which he can express himself. Children worship through the familiar. They can participate meaningfully only when they know the songs, verses, and other materials which they use. Many materials which have been studied and learned in the class periods may be used to enrich the worship.

Children may create and prepare litanies, prayers, and poems for use in the worship service. These activities take time and can often be carried on in the class groups. Directions for the teacher to follow in guiding such activities will be found in many teacher's books. Older children may help plan the services, and arrange the worship center under the wise guidance of their teachers.

Primary children need careful guidance in prayer. Prayer is a part of worship. For group worship, memorized prayers, prayer songs, and choral responses may be used. Through these songs and prayers, all may participate. They should be a sincere expression of the children's thoughts and feelings and not a mere repetition of words. A prayer which has been developed by a class group may be used to close a session, or it may be used in the worship service whenever it fits the theme of the service.

Prayers for primary children should be simple and brief. They will be offered at the time when there is a readiness for prayer, and they will be the natural expression of the children. Prayer in the class groups may follow a story, conversation, the facing and solving of a problem of conduct, or be used as a climax to an activity or an aesthetic experience.

If the environment is right for a sincere, spontaneous prayer on the part of the child, he may pray aloud. It is unwise to call primary children up before the group, without preparation, and ask them to pray aloud, or to start with a child and go around the class circle asking each child to pray. The child must be willing, feel a need, and have a desire to express his thoughts or feelings to God. This cannot be forced. It must come naturally without self-consciousness on the part of the child. Sometimes the leader or teacher will pray with the children, using her own words. She prays *for* the children in her times of private devotions. She prays *with* them when she is guiding them in worship. The words which she uses should be the words which they can think and feel. Primary children are literal-minded. "Dear God, help us to be happy as we work and worship together this morning," is a prayer which the children may pray as the teacher expresses the words aloud. "Us" and "we" are inclusive. Leader and children are one in the prayer. How much better that is than the prayer which is sometimes used: "Dear God, bless the children. Help them to study and work together this morning"! This type of prayer for the children fails to lead them into an attitude of true worship, for they cannot feel that they are a part of the experience.

The leader's attitude of reverence, her calm and poise, her quiet voice and unhurried manner, her mastery and use of the materials of worship, all help the children to worship. Children are quick to catch and follow the moods of their leaders. Example is more powerful than precept. The leader will be sensitive to the moods of the children and adept at changing her plans. Sometimes children will not be ready for worship and it cannot be forced.

Memorizing Bible Passages

Primary children do not have the ability to find or read many Bible passages. If a verse or short passage is to be read by a child in the worship service, it will be located and read through with the child before the service in order that he may understand and read the passage accurately and with feeling. Because their reading ability is so limited, primary children should memorize the Bible passages which they will use in worship. Often this may be started in the class groups and guidance given by the teachers for completing the memory work at home.

To help primary children memorize Bible passages can be a joy and is surely a privilege to every teacher. Through these materials she is providing for the child's enjoyment, and giving him language for expressions of his feelings in words more beautiful than he himself could frame. The teacher is helping him to appreciate beautiful literature. She also is giving him a guide for his daily living.

The following suggestions may guide teachers in helping primary children to memorize Bible passages:

1. There should be a definite purpose and use for all the Bible materials to be memorized.

2. The Bible materials should be related to other learning experiences.

3. The Bible materials must be within the child's interest and capacity to memorize and understand.

4. The Bible materials should first be presented as a whole for the child to catch the complete thought. The meaning will then be explored and made vivid and vital to the child. The beauty of words and phrases will be discovered and felt. If the passage is longer than one or two verses, it may be memorized a part at a time in thought units rather than by verses, unless a verse contains a complete thought. The child should understand the ideas as well as the words. Pictures, conversation, or a story may be used to interpret and give meaning to the passage.

5. The emphasis should be on appreciation rather than achievement. Because of children's differing mental capacities, it is unfair to give rewards for memorization. The children's satisfaction should

not be found in an award, but in the beauty and a deep appreciation of the meaning of the passage as their own.

6. After the Bible passage is memorized, it should be used again and again in many ways and in relation to many other materials and experiences.

Litanies

A litany is a responsive prayer. It may express thanksgiving, praise, or petition. The children will enjoy creating their own litanies. The creation of a litany will grow out of some other activity or experience. It should be an expression of the children's feelings which have been stimulated by some learning situation.

At the close of a unit of study on the church, a group of first-grade children composed the following litany:

> For our church, a friendly place,
> *Dear God, we thank thee.*
> For friends and helpers who work here,
> *Dear God, we thank thee.*
> For times of work and worship together,
> *Dear God, we thank thee.*
> For children, fathers, mothers, and all who come here,
> *Dear God, we thank thee.*
> For helping us to worship thee and always being near,
> *Dear God, we thank thee.*

The children may compose both the statements and the response, or they may select from several appropriate Bible verses the one which they wish to use as the response. When materials memorized or created by the children are used in the worship services or in other ways, the children find value in having learned or created the material.

Choral Speaking

Primary children will enjoy participating with other members of the group in simple choric speech. What is choral speaking? It is the interpretation of poetic prose or poetry by solo voices or by many voices speaking in unison in small or larger groups. In helping children to learn and use choral speaking, the teacher should keep in mind fidelity of interpretation, phrasing, timing, emphasis of words, beauty of expression, distinct enunciation, and good voice quality.

Poems, words of songs, poetic prose, and Bible passages are excellent materials for choral speaking with primary children.

The teacher first will read the passage in a vital and beautiful way, giving interpretation through her expression and phrasing. She may read it again before it is discussed with the children. The children should discover the meaning of the words, their rhythm or meter, and where emphasis should be placed. Then they should say it with the teacher. Beauty of expression and meaning, not perfection, is to be sought.

Bible passages simple enough for the children to understand may be used for choric speech in the worship service. Children with lighter or smaller voices may be grouped together and those with darker or heavier voices together. Assign parts according to the mood of the words and follow a natural division. Words which carry a mood of joyousness or exaltation will be given by the light voices, those with deeper moods by the dark voices. Occasionally the voice of one child may be used in a solo part, as for example, the angel in Luke 2:10-12.

Primary children like to be a verse-speaking choir, co-operating with each other in expressing the beauty and meaning of Bible verses to help others feel and sense God's nearness and love.

For Further Study

1. Plan your procedure for the next unit of study in the grade which you are teaching. Outline it carefully.

2. What opportunities for fellowship are there in your Primary Department?

3. What are the uses and values of memorized prayer? What are the dangers? Have you had in your class any unfortunate outcomes as a result of using memorized prayers?

4. Review your uses of Bible materials in your class for the past quarter. How many different methods have you used? Plan some new ways of using Bible materials with your children. Plan with them and with your superintendent to use some of these Bible materials in a worship service.

5. Help your children to create a litany growing out of the experiences of the unit of study which you are now using.

CHAPTER 6

Ways of Teaching (Continued)

The Story and the Primary Child

There is no question about the fact that the story is a determining factor in the lives of primary children. It may arouse the feelings and create in the child a desire for better things. It may help the child make wise choices by showing the satisfying results of such choices. It may also help him discover that consequences come because of the choices which one makes and that often one must abide by his choices even though they do not always bring happiness. A child may glean needed knowledge from a story. It may create in him the desire to bring happiness to others. It may clarify concepts, make truth vital, and motivate conduct. Stories may help primary children learn about peoples and customs of other lands. They may lead to appreciation of great art and music, and the worth-while achievements of noble persons. The child may find the solution of some of his problems through a story. A story may develop a sense of humor and help the child have fun. The primary age is the age of action and imagination. Primary children are interested in stories about children of their own age and the things they do. Nature stories and stories that tell the "why" and "how" of things appeal to them. Stories that bring to their imagination experiences in an ever-enlarging world and challenge their thinking also hold interest for them.

Telling the Story

We cannot tell any story effectively unless we have prepared it carefully. Read the story aloud. If it is a Bible story, read it as it is given in the Bible. It is helpful to read it from several translations. Study the story to discover its parts or structure. Mark the introduction, body, climax, and conclusion. This will help you visualize or outline the story in your mind. Live with the characters and participate in the action of the story in your imagination. Read the story again. Then practice telling it. Now you are ready to tell it to the children.

The following suggestions will help you in telling a story in your class session:

1. Remember that a "told" story is more effective than a "read" story.

2. Do not memorize a story. A few phrases or verses or poetry that are used in the story may be memorized, but try always to tell the story in your own words.

3. Use simple, concrete words in telling the story.

4. Use direct discourse wherever possible.

5. Live the story as you tell it.

6. Look into the eyes of your children as you tell it.

7. Tell the story vividly, but do not overdramatize. If gestures are natural, use them, but be sure that they do not detract from the story.

8. If the children should interrupt with a question or remark, overlook it if possible. But make a mental note of it that you may answer it later, if it really needs an answer.

9. Never moralize at the conclusion of the story. If your story is a good one, has been adequately prepared and well told, it will teach its own lesson. If you have to point up the message or moralize, either the story itself is not sound or you have not told it well. Stop when you have finished. The children will catch the message.

10. It should not take much longer than five minutes to tell a story to primary children. Their span of attention is short.

Primary Children May Tell Stories

Primary children enjoy retelling stories which they have heard. One child may tell the complete story. Or the children may tell "stand-up" stories, as one group called them. One child began the story. When another child was ready to continue the story at any point, he stood up. The first child stopped and the second child picked up the story where the first child left off. And so it continued until the story was completed. Primary children like to tell stories using dolls or puppet figures, moving them about on a low table or in a puppet theater. One child may speak for each character in the story.

Pictures illustrating a story may be arranged on cards in sequence. The teacher holds up the first picture with the invitation: "Who can tell this story? Begin here." A child tells the part of the story which the first picture illustrates. The teacher then shows the next picture and a child tells that part, and so on until the story is finished.

Figures to illustrate the characters or animals of a story may be cut from black construction paper or cardboard and fastened to pieces of wood about the size of a foot ruler. These will serve as handles. The children may stand behind a screen and move the figures across the top as they tell the story. If the story is worked out in scenes and dialogue, the children may speak as the characters. This is a form of dramatization.

Dramatization

As a teaching tool, dramatization is highly effective with primary children, for we are utilizing their natural characteristics. The primary child likes to act. He is imitative, and play is his natural world. Dramatization may awaken creativity and the child's ability to express himself. If used carefully it gives the child self-confidence. It stimulates imagination, releases emotions, builds attitudes, and helps the child solve his own problems as he plays the part of someone who has a similar problem. Dramatization often crystallizes the message of the story.

In using dramatization as a method of teaching primary children, we are concerned most with what is happening to the children and what they are learning. The audience, if there is one, is of secondary importance. Primary children will seldom dramatize before an audience except of children their own age. Whenever dramatization is used, it should be related to the session and help fulfill the purposes of the unit. The dramatization may grow out of or lead into other activities.

There are a number of forms of dramatization which are helpful for primary children:

1. The *dramatization of a story* is the form most often used. A story which is suitable for dramatization must have a sound structure, involve action throughout, and contain much direct discourse. It should portray Christian principles of behavior and deal with experiences within the understanding of the child. The story must be so well told that the plot, characters, and setting of the story are vivid and clear. Direct discourse should be used as much as possible,

for this will help the children to work out the scenes and dialogue. Primary children should dramatize spontaneously and freely. Their dramatizations may consist of several short scenes. They will plan simple dialogue. They should try out each scene a number of times, talk about it, and do it over again.

2. *Pantomime* is another form of dramatization which primary children enjoy. As the teacher or a child tells the story, other children may act it out in pantomime, expressing the action without words. Or a child may play that he is doing something to help at home or school, and the other children may try to guess what he is doing.

3. The *spontaneous dramatic play* of primary children is the medium through which they relive things which have happened and try out new ways of living. The child also works off tensions and releases emotions and resentments through his dramatic play. The teacher should plan time for some free play in the class session, whenever possible.

4. *Picture posing* is a form of dramatization. After the children have studied and talked about a picture, such as *The Angelus* or *Feeding Her Birds* by Millet, they may wish to pose the picture. This intensifies the message of the picture and deepens their appreciation of it.

5. Primary children may create their own *plays*. These will be simple and very short, but this activity stimulates thinking and develops imagination.

6. *Hand puppets* and *silhouette figures* are excellent media for the dramatization of a story. They may be moved by handles extending above, at the side, or below the figures, with the children speaking for the characters.

Elaborate costumes and scenery are not essential when primary children dramatize. Simple ones may be made and used, but these children will carry dramatizations through without the aid of costumes or scenery.

Conversation

Conversation is used with primary children to help them share experiences and information and to develop self-confidence and self-control through listening and taking turns in speaking. It may stimulate creative thinking. If we are to be successful in the use of this method with primary children, we must respect each child as an individual and have regard for the contributions which he makes. A feeling of friendly sharing, seeking answers, and exploring interesting subjects should permeate the conversation period. The teacher will listen to what the children have to say and show evidence of real interest in it.

Informal conversation is not a question-and-answer period in which the teacher asks a question of each child in turn and receives answers. Something of interest to all is introduced by a child or teacher, and the group talks about it informally, each one making his contributions, asking questions and exchanging ideas as interest leads. The teacher guides skillfully so that the conversation is purposeful and worth while.

The teacher should help each child to respect the contributions of the other children. She is alert to help every child participate and to see that no child monopolizes the time and attention. Questions should be stated directly and simply. Questions that can be answered with "yes" or "no," or which suggest the answer, do not stimulate thinking. The best teaching helps children think. Conversation can do this.

Informal conversation is especially valuable as the children arrive, for then they will be eager to share with the teacher interesting things that happened during the week. These may give the teacher insight into the children's thoughts and feelings and help her discover their needs. Conversation may be used in the class session for review, making plans or evaluating work done. The children may be called together in the midst of an activity to talk over further plans or solve some difficulty which has arisen and clarify plans and responsibilities. Children enjoy talking about pictures and songs. They can talk about trips before they go and when they return.

Where there is understanding and wholesome respect for each other and for each other's ideas, freedom of conversation will abound, and teacher and children will have through it many joyous learning experiences together.

Creative Activities

Activities, if they are to be most helpful for primary children, should be as creative as possible. To create means to produce something new out of existing materials. The children engage in activities which produce new insights, appreciations, skills, or habits. Does this mean that we will never use with primary children patterns or pictures to color? Yes, if the patterns are not purposeful and do not contribute to the child's growth. Too often patterns are only time-fillers or busy work. Many times patterns or activity materials fail of their purpose, not because the planning in the teacher's material for its use was not adequate, but because the teacher herself fails to relate it to the session plans and purposes.

Creative writing is an excellent form of expressing ideas. Primary children may create litanies, psalms, music, class prayers, poems, verses for songs, stories, and notes or invitations. They must have something to express. Such creative work is not made on demand, but grows out of guided thinking and the child's experience. Creative writing cannot be hurried. A child's imagination and experience, an atmosphere of unhurried freedom, and an alert teacher may bring into being many lovely pieces of children's writing.

Drawing, painting, finger-painting, clay modeling, and paper cutting provide opportunities for the child to express ideas through his hands. A group of first-grade children had been thinking of God's gifts. Each child was drawing a picture of the gift for which he was most thankful. When the teacher came to Roddy, she could not tell what he was making, so her only comment was on the lovely colors which he had used. A little later the teacher came again to Roddy's place just as he finished the picture. He looked up at her and said, "And this is the star." Of course, there was the stable, Mary leaning over the Christ child in the manger, and the shepherds. God's gifts! Yes, God's best gift to the world—that was the expression of Roddy's thinking. Would it not have been too bad if the teacher had given the children just outline pictures of flowers or fruit to color? Let the children express their own ideas in their own ways. The colors may be smeared some and the objects have little form, but if it is the child's own work it has value for him.

The making of wall murals, posters, dioramas, movies, and large models of objects are most worth-while group activities in which all of the children may have a part in the planning and work.

Primary children should see and feel the value of each activity. They should be able to complete it with a feeling of satisfaction.

An uncompleted activity loses much of its teaching value. Occasionally primary children may choose and insist on doing something that the teacher knows is too difficult for them. If this happens and the activity cannot be completed, the teacher should help the children discover why. Then the children will not have a sense of failure, but may be led to discover that unwise choices many times bring unsatisfactory consequences.

Friendship Enterprises

A primary child has not grown as he should in Christian attitudes and relationships to others until he expresses these through action. Through enterprises of service and friendship primary children may develop attitudes and actions of thoughtfulness and consideration for others. They may grow in their appreciation of other people, of God as the Creator of all, of themselves as members of the world family, and of their part in bringing happiness to others.

For an enterprise to be of the greatest value it should be as concrete and personal as possible. It should be possible for the children to complete it and have a sense of fellowship with others in so doing. Children can recognize needs and help to meet them if the needs are near enough to their own experience. A child may be eager to do something for a sick playmate, for he knows what sickness means. The primary child will find satisfaction in service enterprises within his own group, the church, school, and neighborhood. Other friendship enterprises may be missionary projects that are world-wide in their outreach.

The enterprise should be chosen by the children and one which they really desire to do, not one which the teacher imposes on them. The teacher may first know the need, but she will so guide the children that they choose and have a deep desire to carry the enterprise through. Many of these friendly enterprises will grow out of the graded lesson units; some may grow out of a need that arises in a class; and others may grow out of a reported or discovered need elsewhere. These enterprises may range all the way from cheer cards or gifts to a sick member of the class to school packets or boxes to mission stations. Primary children often will have a part in an enterprise that is shared by the entire church, such as a Thanksgiving or Christmas project, or the support of a doctor in a mission hospital.

Most graded courses include missionary units. In addition, each year two mission studies, one foreign and one home, are provided for primary children through your denomination's missionary agency. These follow the same theme as the current missionary materials which are used by other groups in the church. An illustrated children's book and a leader's guide are provided. The stories in the children's book may be read by the children, or be told by the teacher as a series of stories in worship services or class periods. The leader's guide offers suggestions for the use of the stories, lists additional resource materials, and describes many friendly enterprises.

All friendly enterprises and missionary activities of primary children should be part of the ongoing program of Christian education in the Primary Department. Some of the enterprises may be carried through in the expanded session, which offers more time. A simple dedication service for their gifts will add value for the children.

Trips

Not all teaching takes place in the classroom, nor need it do so. One of the ways to make learning and knowledge concrete is to take the children to see the thing about which they have been studying.

A group of primary children were learning about God's laws of nature. On a snowy morning they made a trip to a near-by park where they caught snowflakes on pieces of dark cloth and looked at them through a magnifying glass. They were seeking two snowflakes just alike. Finally Elmer said, "Do you suppose if we caught a hundred million of them, we could find two alike?"

"I don't know that anyone has ever caught a hundred million snowflakes, but no one has ever found two alike," the teacher replied.

Holding his arms wide, and with his face uplifted, Elmer said, "There must be a hundred million snowflakes coming down right here. Just think what God can do."

No amount of talking, peering through windows, or looking at pictures could have led to the moments of discovery and wonder which that trip outdoors had brought.

Trips to the church sanctuary, to other departments, to a sick friend or shut-in, to community centers of interest, art exhibits and institutions all may contribute to Christian growth.

If children are to take a trip there must be careful preparation before they go. The teacher will plan with the children. If they are to go where other people are involved, as to the home of a shut-in, the teacher should contact these persons in advance to prepare them for the coming of the children. She also will let them know the purpose of the trip. She should be alert at all

times during the trip to recognize and use teaching situations. Upon the return from the trip, children and teacher should talk over and evaluate the experience.

Other Ways of Teaching

Many other valuable ways of teaching have already been described in chapter 4. For suggestions on using Bible material refer back to pages 51-53. The use of pictures is discussed on pages 55-57, music and songs on pages 57-59, poems on pages 59-60, projected and nonprojected materials on pages 61-62.

Workers Needed with Primary Children

The number of workers needed in the Primary Department will depend upon the organization of the department, the number of children, and the available space.

In a small church in which there are less than twelve children of primary age, one class that meets in a space provided for them for the entire session will be sufficient. The teacher keeps the records, leads the worship, and conducts the class activities.

If there is a large number of primary children, a department superintendent, secretary, pianist, and a teacher for each group of eight to twelve children will be needed. There should be one or more classes for children of six, seven, and eight years old. It is not necessary nor desirable to place boys and girls in separate classes. The children meet together for worship and separately for class periods.

If there is available space, and from fifteen to thirty children of each grade, there are two possible plans. Each grade may be organized as a department with a superintendent, secretary, pianist, and a teacher for each class; or each grade may be organized as one large class. A supervisory teacher with as many assistants as she needs for various phases of the work will carry through the complete program for the entire session. This plan requires fewer but more skillful teachers.

The Superintendent

The superintendent of the Primary Department should be informed about, and in touch at all times with, the total church program for Christian education. She notes its implications for the primary children and represents the teachers and children in carrying out the phase of the program which relates to the Primary Department.

The superintendent is the key person in establishing and maintaining wholesome working relationships between all persons within the department. She should be a person of sympathetic understanding and should be able to see all persons and all situations objectively.

The superintendent leads the formal worship service. She should consult with the teachers about any contributions which a class may make in the service. She encourages and uses all contributions of the children. She may ask a class to prepare a special part for the service. She knows what is being done in the different classes at all times.

The superintendent may find and recommend teachers for appointment. She should plan and conduct the departmental conferences in which she and the teachers plan for the children. She should help new teachers find and use resource materials, understand purposes and plans, and prepare teaching plans. She should plan and make available training opportunities through classes, books, and conferences. She should work with the teachers for the continuing improvement of the teaching situation, including rooms and materials. The fellowship which new teachers have with more experienced teachers when they plan the work together is one means of teacher growth, or "learning on the job." She should consult with the department secretary about the materials and supplies needed for the children and teachers.

The superintendent and teachers will plan and carry through a program of home visitation, parent contacts, days when the parents shall visit the department, and parent-teacher meetings, to promote closer co-operation between the home and the church.

The Pianist

The pianist is an important worker in the Primary Department. Not every pianist can play satisfactorily for children. Her playing can either help or hinder the children's worship experiences. She should play accurately and with feeling. Before the session begins, she should become thoroughly familiar with the songs, responses, and music for fellowship and worship. The pianist will co-operate with the superintendent, and be regular in attendance and on time. She should be a growing person—in her personal religious living, in her understanding of children, and in her knowledge and appreciation of music and its place and value in the lives of the children.

The Secretary

The secretary of the Primary Department cares for and orders supplies after consultation with the superintendent and teachers. She should keep the attendance records and make out all reports. She should enroll the children and keep accurate, up-to-date information about each child. The secretary should attend all departmental workers' meetings. A good secretary is indispensable.

The Parents

Throughout this book we have called attention to the necessity for close co-operation between the church and the parents. It is important for the primary workers always to remember that the parents are teachers also. The primary workers should constantly be seeking opportunities for a growing understanding and closer work with the parents through every possible means.

The Teacher

It has been said that curriculum is 90 per cent teacher. When we think of the broader meaning of curriculum, the above statement takes on tremendous meaning. What the teacher herself is, feels, and thinks permeates all that she does. Her attitudes toward the church and its program are important. Her relationship to God and Jesus shows through what she is and what she does, even more than through what she says. If she is a sincere Christian, her life confronts her children with the Christian gospel. To lead a child to God, a teacher must know the way herself. She must be what she expects her children to be.

A teacher or leader of primary children should:

1. Be a sincere Christian in the fullest implications of that word, living and reflecting the spirit of Jesus Christ.

2. Be growing in her knowledge, understanding, and appreciation of the Bible and its meaning for her life, as her source of inspiration and guidance for living.

3. Have a clear understanding and a deep sense of mission concerning her teaching; be one who for the love of Christ and loyalty to him knows and feels herself called to guide her children in Christian ways.

4. Be sincerely appreciative of children and the contributions which they make.

5. Have a knowledge and sympathetic understanding of children, based on their worth as persons and their need for spiritual guidance; and be willing to give her best thought and effort when preparing for teaching, when calling in their homes, and when having fellowship with them.

6. Be a well-integrated personality and attractive to children.

7. Be courteous, quiet in manner and voice.

8. Be energetic and enthusiastic.

9. Be friendly, patient, and kind.

10. Work in harmony with the other adults in the department and in the church and be loyal to the church program.

11. Be well informed, have an open mind, and be ready to experiment with new materials and methods of teaching.

12. Be resourceful in finding and using needed materials, keeping her plans flexible enough to meet needs and situations as they arise.

13. Be dependable and regular in preparation and attendance at the church school sessions and workers' conferences.

Every teacher who is worthy of her calling is often overwhelmed with a sense of inadequacy for her task. A teacher's chief concern should not be with what she is at this moment, but should center on how she is growing in her Christian life and in her knowledge and skill as a teacher.

Growing as a Person. There are many opportunities for teachers to grow in their personal religious living. A few of these are briefly suggested here:

1. A definite plan and time for daily devotions.

2. Cultivating a positive approach to life, developing courage, poise, and ability to meet each crisis and experience in a Christian way.

3. Regular participation in the church worship services.

4. Association and fellowship with persons of high ideals and noble actions.

5. Reading inspirational books.

6. An increasing awareness of God's presence in daily living.

7. Development of a sense of humor and the ability to see ings in their true perspective.

8. Growing in understanding of children. (Read again this section in chapter 1, page 19.)

Growing in Teaching Skill. Every teacher should be constantly on the alert to find ways of improving her teaching skill. Good books and magazines that bear on the methods of teaching will be helpful. Some of these are listed in the bibliography at the close of this chapter.

Attendance at workers' conferences and teachers' institutes will prove helpful. Regular departmental workers' meetings, when the workers in the Primary Department gather together to pray, study, and plan for their work, are an imperative for effective growth in teaching. Planning for the year's work, for Christmas, for Easter, for introducing a new unit of study, and for service enterprises are just a few of the matters which might be considered in departmental conferences.

Enrollment and participation in Leadership Education classes or a home study course will also promote growth. Find out what your own denomination has to offer.

It is helpful to invite a supervisory teacher to visit the class and talk over the plans and activities after the class session. A visit to another class or department in another school will give practical ideas and suggestions, and also will help teachers to understand teacher-pupil relationships and will acquaint them with techniques for handling children.

One of the most valuable means of growth is attendance and participation in a laboratory school. Inquire at your denominational office or at a Council of Churches about such a school in your locality.

A teacher can help herself to grow by planning well in advance for her class session, and then, after the session is over, making notes and evaluating her plans in the light of what happened.

It is important for every teacher to have a definite plan for a program of growth, not attempting too many things at one time, but choosing one or two goals which she can reach this year. Next year she can set higher goals and consistently move onward and upward.

"Not that I have already obtained this or am already perfect; but I press on to make it my own, because Christ Jesus has made me his own. Brethren, I do not consider that I have made it my own; but one thing I do, forgetting what lies behind and straining forward to what lies ahead, I press on toward the goal for the prize of the upward call of God in Christ Jesus" (Phil. 3:12-14).

For Further Study

1. Determine the specific purposes of the activities which you will be using in your next unit of study. Check over the supplies that are available. Are they adequate to carry out the activities?

2. How will Bible and other stories be used in your next class session? Plan to follow the suggestions given here for preparing these stories for telling.

3. What are the values of dramatization for primary children? Make a definite plan to help your children dramatize a story or pose a picture.

4. In what service enterprises are your children engaging? What evidences of their growth in relationship to others have you discovered?

5. Study the organization of your department. Is it the most effective for your situation? Do you have enough workers? What plans are under way for securing and training additional workers?

6. Outline your own program of growth for the next year.

Helpful Books and Pamphlets

Books

The Children We Teach, Elizabeth S. Whitehouse
The Child from Five to Ten, Arnold Gesell and F. L. Ilg
Knowing Children Better, Hazel A. Lewis
Heaven in My Hand, Alice L. Humphreys
Angels in Pinafores, Alice L. Humphreys
Guiding Children in Christian Growth, Mary A. Jones
The Faith of Our Children, Mary A. Jones
Our Church Plans for Children, Lois Blankenship, Revised, 1958
Primary Children Learn at Church, Ethel L. Smither
The Primary Church School, Hazel A. Lewis
The Use of Music in Christian Education, Vivian S. Morsch
The Use of the Bible with Children, Ethel L. Smither
Opening the Bible to Children, Elizabeth S. Whitehouse
You Can Do It, Compiled by Margaret M. Clemens
As Children Worship, Jeanette E. Perkins
More Children's Worship in the Church School, Jeanette Perkins Brown
Creative Activities, Rebecca Rice
Here's How and When, Armilda B. Keiser
Children's Worship in the Church School, Jeanette Perkins Brown
Let's Play a Story, Elizabeth Allstrom
The Church: The Gifted and the Retarded Child, Charles F. Kemp
The Spiritual Growth of Children, Dorothy Fritz
Missionary Education of Children, Frances M. Hill

Pamphlets

Objectives for the Christian Education of Children
Your Child Grows Toward God, Pearl Rosser
Rewards and Prizes, Lillian M. Boyd
The Expanded Session, Lois Blankenship
Interpreting Death to Children, Lewis Sherrill
Christmas with Primary Children, Grace Turley
Easter with Primary Children, Winifred A. Baker